Open Access Resources

SPEC Kits

Supporting Effective Library Management for Over Thirty Years

Committed to assisting research and academic libraries in the continuous improvement of management systems, ARL has worked since 1970 to gather and disseminate the best practices for library needs. As part of its commitment, ARL maintains an active publications program best known for its SPEC Kits. Through the Collaborative Research/Writing Program, librarians work with ARL staff to design SPEC surveys and write publications. Originally established as an information source for ARL member libraries, the SPEC series has grown to serve the needs of the library community worldwide.

What are SPEC Kits?

Published six times per year, SPEC Kits contain the most valuable, up-to-date information on the latest issues of concern to libraries and librarians today. They are the result of a systematic survey of ARL member libraries on a particular topic related to current practice in the field. Each SPEC Kit contains an executive summary of the survey results; survey questions with tallies and selected comments; the best representative documents from survey participants, such as policies, procedures, handbooks, guidelines, Web sites, records, brochures, and statements; and a selected reading list—both print and online sources—containing the most current literature available on the topic for further study.

Subscribe to SPEC Kits

Subscribers tell us that the information contained in SPEC Kits is valuable to a variety of users, both inside and outside the library. SPEC Kit purchasers use the documentation found in SPEC Kits as a point of departure for research and problem solving because they lend immediate authority to proposals and set standards for designing programs or writing procedure statements. SPEC Kits also function as an important reference tool for library administrators, staff, students, and professionals in allied disciplines who may not have access to this kind of information.

SPEC Kits can be ordered directly from the ARL Publications Distribution Center. To order, call **(301) 362-8196**, fax **(301) 206-9789**, e-mail **pubs@arl.org**, or go to **http://www.arl.org/resources/pubs/**.

Information on SPEC Kits and the SPEC survey program can be found at **http://www.arl.org/resources/pubs/spec/index.shtml**. The executive summary for each kit after December 1993 can be accessed free of charge at **http://www.arl.org/resources/pubs/spec/complete.shtml**.

SPEC Kit 300

Open Access Resources

September 2007

Anna K. Hood

Head, Serials and Electronic Resources

Kent State University

ASSOCIATION OF RESEARCH LIBRARIES

Series Editor: Lee Anne George

SPEC Kits are published by the

Association of Research Libraries
21 Dupont Circle, NW, Suite 800
Washington, DC 20036-1118
P (202) 296-2296 F (202) 872-0884
http://www.arl.org/spec/
pubs@arl.org

ISSN 0160 3582

ISBN 1-59407-793-2
978-1-59407-793-7

SPEC
Kit 300

Open Access Resources

September 2007

SURVEY RESULTS

REPRESENTATIVE DOCUMENTS

Newsletter Articles and Blogs

Institutional Support for OA Authors

OA Collection Development Policies

Selecting and Cataloging OA Resources

Institutional Repositories

SELECTED RESOURCES

SURVEY RESULTS

EXECUTIVE SUMMARY

Background

Faced with ever-increasing journal subscription costs and declining library collections budgets, libraries are expanding their collections by making open access (OA) research literature available through their catalogs, Web sites, open URL resolvers, and other resources. While not free to produce, as defined by the Budapest Open Access Initiative (BOAI), this literature is freely accessible to users. Providing access to these resources lends support to the open access movement and serves students, faculty, and staff by connecting them to an important body of scholarly output. Although some libraries have embraced OA literature and have fully integrated it into their selection, acquisition, and cataloging processes, others have been less active in this area.

The purpose of this survey was to gather information on whether and how ARL member libraries are selecting, providing access to, cataloging, hosting, tracking usage of, and promoting the use of open access research literature for their patrons by using established library resources such as the OPAC and link resolvers. It was hoped the survey results would provide valuable information for those libraries interested in incorporating OA content into their collections.

The survey was sent to the 123 ARL member libraries in March 2007. Seventy-one responses were received by the deadline, a return rate of 58%. All but one of the survey respondents provide access to OA resources. These 70 libraries represent 57% of the ARL membership.

Linking and Hosting

The survey asked to which kinds of open access resources the library provides links for users. Sixty-nine respondents (97%) provide links to journals, the category most commonly associated with the open access movement. Sixty-two (87%) provide links to government documents, literature that is typically available without charge. A majority provides access to monographs or theses / dissertations (80%), followed by conference papers / proceedings or technical reports (62%). A little more than a third provide access to legal documents. While the BOAI definition of open access literature primarily encompasses journal articles, respondents apparently use a broader definition. Forty-one percent link to OA resources that include digitized photos, maps, and other images, video and audio files, statistical and geospatial data, and other resources that are not scholarly writing. This is not unexpected, as these all belong to the broader class of freely available electronic resources. Fifty-two of the responding libraries (74%) host OA resources on their own servers.

Libraries are using multiple channels to provide links to OA resources. Survey respondents commonly provide access to locally hosted OA resources of all types through OPAC records (82%), Web pages (70%), and institutional repositories

(56%). For journal articles, they also use open URL resolvers, a third-party title list or portal such as Serials Solutions or EBSCO, and electronic resource management systems. For externally hosted titles, they most often use OPAC records (94%), open URL resolvers (79%), Web pages, (73%), or a third-party title list or portal (67%). As one respondent explained, they use "all the same channels as non-OA resources."

The survey asked for an approximate number of OA titles linked to. Many respondents noted the difficulty or impossibility of providing counts of titles by specific categories. However, from those who attempted an estimate, the three types of locally hosted resources with the highest median title counts were government documents (15,050 titles), theses and dissertations (493), and technical reports (170). The externally hosted resources with the highest median title counts were government documents (37,155), theses and dissertations (3,500), journals (3,102), and legal documents (2,000).

Selection and Financial Support

Most of the responding libraries (84%) do not have collection development policies that specifically address criteria for selecting externally hosted OA resources, though several libraries report that collection development policies are undergoing revision and there are plans or desires to address OA resources in their policies. Typically, the selection criteria (79%) and the selectors (91%) for externally hosted OA resources are the same as for other electronic resources. Some libraries provide access to all titles in the Directory of Open Access Journals (DOAJ) rather than making title-level decisions.

Because they are usually not supported by subscription fees, many open access journals get their funding through fees paid by authors or their institutions. These author fees are often paid by libraries at the author's institution. The majority of responding libraries (68%) provide financial support for externally hosted OA journals, either directly or through a consortium. Many contribute to BioMed

Central, Public Library of Science (PLoS), and the Stanford Encyclopedia of Philosophy, among others. Only a few (36%) provide financial support for internally hosted OA journals. Although some don't provide direct financial support for these resources, they do provide staff time and support for processing.

Cataloging

For externally hosted OA resources, the most popular methods of obtaining catalog records are downloading records from OCLC (86%), creating original, full records in the library (69%), and acquiring records from another third party such as Serials Solutions (56%). About a third also create original, brief records or acquire them from other libraries such as consortial partners. Catalog records for locally hosted OA resources are most commonly obtained by creating original, full records (87%), creating original, brief records (56%), and downloading records from OCLC (42%). Other methods of obtaining descriptive data for both locally and externally hosted OA resources include the automated harvesting of XML metadata, records created by the authors, brief records created by an electronic resource management system (ERM), and records provided by the publishers. In all but three of the responding libraries (95%), the staff who create catalog records for OA resources are the same staff who create records for other electronic resources.

Although two libraries report spending 100 to 120 hours per month cataloging OA resources, most spend fewer than 20 hours per month. Others don't track the time. Several respondents pointed out that cataloging of OA material was a very minor portion of cataloging work, perhaps less than 1% of total time spent on cataloging. Others emphasized that they did not treat the cataloging of OA resources differently than non-OA resources—catalogers simply integrate work with these material into their usual workload. In many libraries, both professional catalogers and support staff create catalog records. Most of the libraries (89%) that create original records for OA resources contribute them to OCLC. Of the libraries that include links to OA resources in the OPAC, 40% identify these records by some kind of field or tag. These fields include source of acquisition (039), electronic location and access (856), notes, and added entries for title (730, 793), series (including locally created series statements) and author (usually corporate), as well as indications in holdings records. Host item entry (773) was used by at least one library to identify open access resources.

Link Maintenance and Usage Tracking

As with other electronic resources, records for OA resources require ongoing maintenance. URLs in catalog records, Web sites, and other tools quietly become outdated every day. Almost all of the libraries (90%) respond to reports of problems with links and many (64%) rely on a data provider (such as Serials Solutions) for link checking. Some libraries (33%) use third-party software or scripts for link checking, while others (21%) use locally developed solutions, a few use manual checking, ILS link checking software or some other method. Not all libraries do link checking; 19 (28%) report that they don't systematically monitor or maintain links locally.

Link checking software used by respondents includes software from integrated library system vendors such as Innovative Interfaces and Endeavor (5 libraries), OCLC PURL link checker software (3), Xenu (3), LinkBot (2), JTurl (1), and LinkScan (1). Many respondents noted that the URLs of OA resources were less stable than those of subscription resources and that OA resources sometimes change from free to paid or simply disappear. OA resources can take longer than subscription resources to resolve access problems and may be down more frequently than purchased resources. However, non-OA resources also require their share of link maintenance.

Libraries can spend a great deal of time tracking the use of resources that they purchase. Many are also interested in the return on the investment they make to select, process, and promote OA resources. Slightly fewer than half of the respondents (46%) track the usage of internally hosted OA resources; a little more than half (55%) track usage of externally hosted OA resources. For locally hosted resources, usage data is provided by repository software and server logs. For other OA resources, usage data is acquired from open URL resolvers such as SFX, from Serials Solutions, and from other sources.

Promotion

While 75% of the survey respondents report that they don't promote OA resources differently than other resources, they still actively alert library users to the availability of OA resources and help staff and users understand what they are. In addition to simply listing OA resources in library catalogs, many (79%) include OA resources in pathfinders or subject guides. Others discuss OA resources during instruction sessions (54%) or in newsletter articles (48%); promote them using library Web pages (46%); discuss them during the reference interview (45%); and send e-mail alerts about newly available OA resources (36%). Other methods include campus forums and contacting faculty by means of flyers, meetings, etc. One respondent commented that they must promote OA resources more than traditional resources because they are relatively new. On the other hand, several respondents said they promote paid resources more than OA resources; OA resources have a lower priority in general and libraries have a hard enough time getting patrons to use paid resources.

Conclusion

Many of the responding libraries are actively educating faculty and students about open access and other issues in scholarly communication through Web sites, newsletters, and blogs. Efforts are made to provide introductory material on open access as well as portals for further research participation, or utilization of open access materials. Many institutions have made formal statements in support of open access efforts. Some include detailed information on author fees and any institutional support or discounts available for authors publishing in open access journals.

In addition to providing access to externally hosted OA resources, libraries also host OA resources on their own servers. Locally hosted OA resources include digital collections and archives, pre-publication material, lectures, primary source material, finding aids, theses and dissertations, grey literature, Web sites, and databases, in addition to journals. As with print collections, libraries provide storage, access, and maintenance for these digital collections.

For some libraries, OA titles are fully integrated into their procedures for selection, processing, and promotion, and typically the selection of these titles is treated no differently than the acquisition of any other material. In a few libraries, time constraints prevent them from assigning a significant priority to OA resources. Regardless of whether libraries choose to distinguish between OA and traditional, subscription-supported resources when selecting and processing materials, libraries face practical challenges in providing access to and information about OA for their users.

SURVEY QUESTIONS and RESPONSES

The SPEC survey on Open Access Resources was designed by **Anna K. Hood**, Head, Serials and Electronic Resources, Kent State University. These results are based on data submitted by 71 of the 123 ARL member libraries (58%) by the deadline of March 12, 2007. The survey's introductory text and questions are reproduced below, followed by the response data and selected comments from the respondents.

As defined by the Budapest Open Access Initiative, open access research literature has "free availability on the public Internet, permitting any users to read, download, copy, distribute, print, search, or link to the full texts of these articles, crawl them for indexing, pass them as data to software, or use them for any other lawful purpose, without financial, legal, or technical barriers other than those inseparable from gaining access to the Internet itself."

As the BOAI public statement puts it, "[p]rimarily, this category encompasses...peer-reviewed journal articles, but it also includes any unreviewed preprints that [scholars] might wish to put online for comment or to alert colleagues to important research findings." It does not include books from which their authors would prefer to generate revenue. It does not include any non-scholarly writings, such as novels or news.

While the BOAI does not specifically cover donated scholarship other than peer-reviewed journal articles and preprints, it could be extended quite naturally to all the writings for which authors do not expect payment. These include scholarly monographs on specialized topics, conference proceedings, theses and dissertations, government reports, and statutes and judicial opinions.

Much of the literature on open access content deals with aspects of publication (i.e., business models, sustainability, and distribution), author-participation, and peer review of content. However, the literature is relatively silent on addressing the practical challenges libraries face in providing access to open access content.

The purpose of this survey is to gather information on whether and how ARL member libraries are selecting, providing access to, cataloging, hosting, tracking usage of, and/or promoting discovery of open access literature for their users by using established library resources such as the OPAC and link resolvers to serve as gateways/facilitators to open access resources. This survey will provide valuable information for those libraries eager to incorporate OA content into their established workflow.

BACKGROUND

1. Please indicate to which kinds of open access (OA) resources your library provides links for library users. Check all that apply. N=71

Journals	69	97%
Government documents	62	87%
Monographs	57	80%
Theses and dissertations	57	80%
Technical reports	44	62%
Conference papers/proceedings	44	62%
Legal documents	24	34%
Other resource, please specify	29	41%
Library does not provide links to OA resources	1	1%

Other resources include:

Audio, graphic, text, and numeric databases

Databases, Web sites

Digital Archives

Digital exhibits, datasets, oral history transcripts, videos, images

Digitized collections from our and other libraries and archives

Free databases, such as MedlinePlus, Movie database, AllMusic, Notable KY African Americans, etc.

Historical photographs, Heritage Collection

Image repositories

Images, image collections, indexing services, finding aids, manuscripts, statistical data, geospatial data

Indexes, Databases

Learning objects, archival materials

Lectures

Local scholarly output

Locally published digital resources

Major digital collections or resources, such as Valley of the Shadow and Stanford Encyclopaedia of Philosophy

Monographs: NGO reports, National Academy Press. Others: databases (e.g. Middle English compendium, cartographic materials)

Our locally digitized materials are all open access.

Preprints, A&I databases, search engines/portals

Pre-publications, research reports

Speeches

Video, field notes, audio files, maps

Web casts

Working papers, syllabi, scores, manuscripts, photographs

2. **Does your library host any OA resources on its own servers? N=70**

Yes	52	74%
No	18	26%

3. Through what channel(s) does your library provide links to OA resources? Check all that apply. N=70

Locally Hosted Resources N=57

	N	Theses/Dissertations	Journals	Monographs	Technical reports	Government documents	Conference Papers	Legal documents	Other resource
	N	40	39	29	25	25	23	10	34
OPAC records	47	30	29	25	11	18	8	5	15
Library Web page	40	16	23	17	9	14	10	7	18
Institutional repository	32	24	17	15	19	6	13	2	17
Open URL resolver	18	1	15	2	2	3	2	2	1
A third-party title list or portal (e.g., Serials Solutions, EBSCO)	14	1	11	1	3	3	4	2	—
Electronic Resource Management (ERM) system	11	1	10	4	2	4	2	1	3
Other channel	10	5	2	4	2	3	1	1	6

Please specify other resource(s) in:

OPAC

American Memory, Global Gateway, Thomas, Country Studies, etc.

Databases, Web sites

Digital archives

Digital collections

Digitized historical collections

Free databases

Image collections, statistical databases, geospatial data

Image repositories

Images

Learning objects, archival materials

Local projects

Pamphlets

Sponsored research reports

ERM

Databases

Free Databases

Web Page

College catalogs

Database locator

Databases, Web sites

Digital archives

Digital collections

Digital exhibits

Digital photo collection

Free databases

Image collections, statistical databases, geospatial data

Images

Local Projects

Institutional Repository

College catalogs

Data sets, oral history transcripts, videos, images

Department documents/working papers, etc

Digital Commons @ Mac

Images, finding aids, manuscripts

Journal articles; book chapters, pre-publications

Learning objects

Lectures

Primary source materials

Sponsored research reports, radio broadcasts, promotional material, grey literature, campus publications

University archives

Web casts

Please specify the other channel for:

Journals

OJS

Monographs

ContentDM

DLG database

Schoenberg Center for Electronic Text and Image

Theses

ContentDM

Dissertation Abstracts Fulltext

LOCKSS

NDLTD

Theses Canada Portal

WorldCat

Government Documents

DLG database

LOCKSS

Digital photo collection; images

ContentDM

Selected Comments from Respondents

"All the same channels as non-OA resources."

"Although not hosted by the Libraries, we have catalogued some e-journals that are locally hosted. The archival collections are locally digitized collections that are catalogued at the collection level only."

"At present, we locally host only several open access journals."

"Currently, the LOCKSS server is being used for the electronic dissertations and theses, but these will be moved over to DSpace this summer (institutional repository)."

"ERM from III is being developed."

"Library Web page: We don't provide direct links from the 'home' page as such, but individual subject specialists do link from their own pages as appropriate."

"Our institutional repository accepts any type or format of publication."

"The ERM is our own in-house product."

"We harvest OAI archive records into our OPAC from a number of sites."

"We have OPAC records for serial titles included in our OA AgEcon subject repository. They are also in SFX and appear on the public SFX generated A-Z list of e-resources. Institutional repository includes selective institutional records and documents."

Externally Hosted Resources N=70

	N	Journals	Government documents	Monographs	Theses/Dissertations	Conference Papers	Technical reports	Legal documents	Other resource
	N	69	61	52	42	39	37	22	22
OPAC records	66	62	60	49	29	33	30	17	12
Open URL resolver	55	54	17	22	6	15	11	5	1
Library Web page	51	42	31	28	19	18	20	17	16
A third-party title list or portal (e.g., Serials Solutions, EBSCO)	47	45	12	9	9	8	2	2	2
Electronic Resource Management (ERM) system	21	19	5	7	2	3	3	2	5
Institutional repository	16	11	2	4	8	7	9	—	6
Other channel	5	1	1	1	5	1	1	1	—

Please specify other resource(s) in:

OPAC

Audio, graphic, and numeric databases

Collections/databases

Databases, Web sites

Digital archives

Free databases

Image collections, statistical databases, geospatial data, manuscripts, indexing services

Indexes & databases

Local scholarly output

MEDLINE; ADS

Third-party Title List

SFX

ERM

Databases

Free databases

MEDLINE; ADS; DOAJ

Open URL Resolver

SFX

Library Web Page

Audio, graphic, and numeric databases

Collections/databases

Databases, Web sites

Digital archives

Digital collections

Free databases

Image collections, statistical databases, geospatial data, manuscripts, indexing services

Image repositories

Indexes & databases

Open access collections such as Valley of Shadow and Stanford Encyclopaedia of Philosophy

Reference guides on other library Web pages

Subject Web pages provide links to a variety of free/open access scholarly resources on the Web

Institutional Repository

Book chapters; speeches

e-Scholarship repository

Local scholarly output

Web casts

Working papers

Selected Comments from Respondents

"Access links interpreted as both individual item links and portal (ex. Arxiv.org)."

"All the same channels as non-OA resources. This is a very difficult question to answer as we generally do not distinguish OA from other resources."

"Legal documents are in the process of being listed on the Law Library Web pages."

"Open access resources (journals and monographs) are profiled in our ERM but not made public through this system."

"Other resource: databases such as MEDLINE/PubMed."

"Our institutional repository is hosted by a remote vendor."

"Our IR is externally hosted."

"We have a separate e-journals section on our Web page that makes DOAJ and other open access journals available through SFX. If a librarian requests that a Web site be cataloged, an OPAC record is created. Commercial databases often contain open access content; we pay for the power of the search engine."

"We've checked many item types for Library Web Page because our link resolver interface ("FindIt") constitutes a Web page that pulls in results including all sorts of document types from our locally and externally held collections, as well as the open Web."

4. What is the approximate number of OA titles to which the library provides links? N=57

Locally Hosted Titles N=36

	N	Minimum	Maximum	Mean	Median	Std Dev
Journals	22	1	2,567	170.4	4.5	575.5
Theses and dissertations	22	13	14,000	2,670.0	493.0	4,003.8
Monographs	14	1	5,000	469.9	45.0	1,316.5
Technical reports	8	4	7,761	1,627.8	170.0	2,854.8
Conference papers	4	2	400	165.3	129.5	197.3
Government documents	4	1	725,000	188,775.3	15,050.0	357,761.9
Legal documents	3	1	150	50.7	1.0	86.0
Other resource	18	1	5,000,000	296,762.2	411.0	1,175,093.0

Please specify other resource.

American Memory

Campus publications

Conference abstracts, images

Department documents, working papers, etc

Digital photo collection

EAD; images; texts; e-texts; statistical & geospatial

Image repositories

Images

Internet sites, archives

Learning objects, archival materials

Loose articles

Pamphlets

Photos, meeting documents

Primary source documents

Speeches

Externally Hosted Titles N=50

	N	Minimum	Maximum	Mean	Median	Std Dev
Journals	46	12	33,284	4,945.5	3,102.5	6,214.7
Monographs	24	3	612,300	29,245.1	929.0	124,376.9
Government documents	22	800	215,000	40,900.4	37,155.0	44,613.1
Theses and dissertations	12	1	17,500	5,282.8	3,500.0	5,753.7
Technical reports	8	10	25,000	5,688.1	77.5	10,462.5
Conference papers	7	20	5,000	1,124.1	83.0	1,934.5
Legal documents	3	71	20,000	7,357.0	2,000.0	10,991.6
Other resource	12	2	1,000,000	84,482.8	42.5	288,324.5

Please specify other resource.

Collections

Databases

Image repositories

Indexes & databases

Internet sites, archives

Maps

Speeches

Working papers

Selected Comments from Respondents

"Although we provide access to government documents, we cannot generate a number for this category of open-access titles. Estimate: c. 40,000."

"Approximate OA journal count is 5733, there is no way for us to distinguish OA from free in our dataset."

"Cannot determine number of external government docs. or ETDs."

"Did not include free books in NetLibrary. If we had not purchased NetLibrary books, our users would not have had access. The digitized archival collections consist of Winnipeg Blg. Index (4,200 items), Arctic Blue Books (4,900), Tribune Photos (7,230), Canadian War Experience (10,000), Prairie Immigration (10,000), Manitoba. ca (200,000). Learning objects: 25."

"I do not have estimate of numbers because done via consortial arrangement."

"Even approximate numbers would be difficult to provide. For example, various library units have digital initiatives where the materials are made public. Each unit would have to be contacted and they in turn might have to guess."

"Figures are very approximate; we don't count open access materials separately, so these are estimates. Our theses are generally open access via Library and Archives Canada, although we don't generally direct our own users to that site. We are a federal and provincial depository library, and so we have links to many open access government documents. We would like to do more, but find it difficult to keep up even with links to the resources we pay for."

"I don't at present (brand new ILS) have any way to count the numbers of open access titles to which we link. Journals number is from our link resolver. Monographs number is a guess."

"If we consider Web links, the number would be in the thousands."

"Items have not been tagged in a systematic way to derive an accurate count."

"Locally hosted resources: our institutional repository contains 622 documents as of February 22; the number is not broken down by document types. "

"Number reported under journal include technical reports and proceedings. The SFX KB was used to find out the number of active free journal collections. Some of those SFX free targets (collections) include journals, technical reports, and conference proceedings. Links to government documents are included in our MARCIVE records."

"Numbers of journals and monographs are difficult to estimate because data identifying titles as open access are often not available in bibliographic records."

"Other than for journals, we have direct links to very few of the other OA resources. When we link to monographs or technical reports, for instance, it is almost always to an externally hosted portal for monographs or technical reports, etc., rather than cataloging or linking directly to a particular instance of a monograph or technical report."

"NB: Our numbers are for items, not titles, as institutional repositories generally do not count their contents by titles included (unless the collections consist only of items easily measured on a title basis, e.g., theses and dissertations)."

"Research Exchange includes back issues of journal titles, individual journal articles, and presentations by individuals."

"Since our collecting is based on value rather than source, we do not track this information."

"Statistics for OA are not kept separately when their access is integrated with that of other materials."

"This is not something we've counted as such, but I have estimated "journals" by including the titles in the DOAJ plus 25%."

"We have links for Open Access titles in all of the above categories; however at this time there is no simple way to count these categories individually."

"We do not distinguish or have figures for open access resources."

"We do not track whether an externally hosted resource is OA or not, so we can not provide those numbers. Our locally hosted numbers do not include any previously published material that was converted as part of our digitization efforts."

We have 2481 URLs in our OPAC which are not restricted to our users only—these are freely available resources of a variety of types, including 1388 DOAJ titles. It is not possible to determine which of the remaining URLs are truly Open Access. These records cover most of the first 6 categories listed above."

SELECTION

5. Does your library's collection development policy specifically address criteria for selecting externally hosted OA resources? N=68

Yes	11	16%
No	57	84%

6. Are the selection criteria for externally hosted OA resources the same as for other electronic resources? N=62

Yes	49	79%
No	13	21%

If no, please explain how they differ.

Selected Comments from Respondents

"Although we do not have anything formal about OA resources in our collection development (CD) policy, the CD Department has worked through criteria which we hope to add to our policy related to OA e-resources added to our OPAC. They include the permanence and reliability of a resource. Currently, subject librarians can choose at their own discretion what to add to their subject guides (which they maintain individually)."

"Because of Google Scholar, PubMed, and MS Academic Live links we've decided to add all Open Access resources available through DOAJ and other resources listed in Serials Solutions in our Open URL resolver, ERM, and OPAC. We decided that we'd look silly trying to explain to our faculty why we weren't subscribing to high quality free publications. Given the number of open access titles in DOAJ, over 2000 at the time, it was quicker to accept all than to have the selectors review all the titles and pick the ones that they wanted."

"Collection Policy Statements are in the process of being revised with respect to selecting electronic resources."

"It depends on the type of resource. Open access journals are treated much the same as other journals. Reports, archives, theses, and other documents harvested from OAI sites are not analyzed with the same criteria as journals."

"Policy needs to be reviewed to reflect current scholarly publication environment."

"The library is in the midst of documenting/creating collection development policies, so it's possible that OA resources might be included in an electronic resources policy."

"There's a separate committee that decides which OA resources are cataloged. Also, from SFX, we link to DOAJ content rather than individually selecting titles."

"To the extent that cataloging services can maintain records, all Directory of Open Access Journals are in the OPAC. This is true for the open-URL resolver as well (package level profiling rather than title-level)."

"We add all DOAJ, etc., not title-by-title selection as we do for purchases."

Additional Comments

"All resources must support teaching, learning, and research at our university. Collection development policies guide the selection of material, without necessarily referring to material type or source."

"Although we try to support the OA concept, we select based on relevance to our user community, regardless of cost model."

"At this point in time, we consider OA resources on the same merits as any other resource being reviewed for acquisition."

"Collection development librarians are able to recommend OA titles be added to the OPAC and subject guides/library Web pages."

"Collection managers make selections on the basis of content and suitability for our users' teaching and research needs. The manner of publication should have no bearing on the selection process."

"Collection policy thus far is format agnostic."

"Criteria are the same except for any criteria that involve pricing."

"Items are selected based on suitability for collection and their support of the university's academic mission. A more formal collection development policy is currently in development."

"OA resources are individually selected by collection managers, except in the case of our link resolver where OA journals are enabled by default."

"Open Access resources must meet the same quality standards as other materials that the library acquires."

"The criteria used are not different. We question though the economic model of some open access resources that transfer the production costs from the authors to the libraries: open access resources are in those cases more expensive than commercial ones. For example, BioMed Central: the more our researchers publish in those journals, the more expensive it is for the libraries."

"The special criteria for online resources relate to technical issues; otherwise the policies deal with subject/level criteria which cover all formats. Open access is not an issue, except in that we can immediately link to desirable OA resources, but may have to delay purchase of restricted ones due to financial constraints."

"We add open access titles to the collection as they become available, when the title is relevant to the collection. The same selection criteria apply to open access titles as to any other library materials."

"We do not differentiate on the basis of funding. We set criteria for content first, with a focus on relevance to our research and teaching. Other criteria follow."

"We link to OA materials (for example DOAJ-listed materials) with no special criteria. Individual subject selectors may have their own criteria for requesting cataloging of OA materials."

"We only add resources to our collection that meet our selection guidelines. The bar is neither higher nor lower for open access materials."

"We select on the basis of potential support for instruction, learning, and research. We consider cost, quality, etc. I would like to develop a systematic approach to selecting OA materials."

7. **Are the library staff who make selection decisions for externally hosted OA resources the same as those who make selection decisions for other electronic resources? N=67**

Yes	61	91%
No	6	9%

If no, please briefly explain who selects OA resources and who selects other electronic resources.

Selected Comments from Respondents

"Catalogers who describe OA resources in the catalog have a greater role, though they select based on recommendations of bibliographers."

"Currently most relevant decisions are by Digital Repository development staff. Policy will become more inclusive in time."

"Final decision about electronic resource purchase is made by collection development librarian (and for bigger purchases the library administration is involved as well). Collection Development Librarian does not get involved in the decision making process for most OA resources, addition of OA resources to library Web site and OPAC is based on liaison's request."

"It is initiated by different staff and handled differently. E-resources staff or others in acquisitions learn of a collection of free resources and ask selectors if they want to add the whole group of resources or not add it. It's all or nothing at this point in time."

"Right now, as we start, a team is identifying resources, but our plan is for department liaisons to be the decision point for including items, once we are further along."

"Sometimes they are the same, but other times due to the large number of records that could be harvested, we do not go through the same process."

8. Does your library provide financial support to any OA journals, including payment of author fees or article processing charges for local faculty, either directly or through a consortium? N=67

	N	Locally Hosted N=50	Externally Hosted N=66
Yes	48	18	45
No	37	32	21

If yes, please briefly explain the type of financial support.

Selected Comments from Respondents

Locally Hosted Only

"Library's journal publications are hosted and are OA."

Externally Hosted Only

"BioMed Central membership. NB: For locally hosted resources, we're not including staff time and support for processing OA resources, but of course there is some cost associated with staff supporting these."

"BioMed Central—Supporters membership (discount to authors); PLoS Active Membership (discount to authors)."

"D-LIB journal, BioMed Central contribution (not author fees)."

"Institutional memberships such as PLos, BioMed Central that provide discounted author's fees for articles accepted for publication."

"Library pays for 'memberships' which allow for discounted author fees for our institutional authors."

"OhioLINK fees."

"The Library is a member of BioMed Central, and pays author/article fees for submissions. We are preparing an institutional repository and will be subsidizing those expenses."

"We are a member of PLOS. We provide a 30% reduction of author fees to faculty if they publish with PLOS."

We provide membership and founding support for some OA resources, e.g., BioMed Central, Stanford Encyclopedia of Philosophy. In some cases we pay 'subscriptions,' e.g., International Journal of Disability and Rehabilitation, Nucleic Acid Research."

"BioMed Central author fees are covered by a consortium group membership with the provider."

"SPARC — charter member support; Vanderbilt TV Archive — initial 2yr sponsor; Stanford Encyclopedia of Philosophy — 3 yr membership; BioMed Central membership — lowers author fees."

"We cover 100% of BioMed Central article processing charge, and through PLoS membership provide 30% for faculty authors. We also indirectly support other OA efforts—by maintaining subscriptions to journals with an OA option and discounts for authors from subscribing institutions."

Both Locally and Externally Hosted

"As an early member of SPARC, we have provided some financial support to the production of SPARC titles. The College Library publishes one e-journal, and absorbs all costs."

"Locally hosted — we host and provide technical support for OA journals connected with faculty/groups at the university. Externally hosted — we have membership fees for OA journals such as BioMed Central and PLoS, which offset the costs of author fees. We contribute funds towards projects such as the Stanford Encyclopedia of Philosophy."

"Locally: library hosts at no charge. Externally: library subsidizes authors' fees."

"PLOS and PNAS discount for authors."

"PubMed Central member; SPARC member."

"SPARC Membership; SSRN Membership (law library); Server and support for locally hosted law journals and ETD repository."

"Support through subscription and/or author fee. We have done this on both the local and consortia level."

"The libraries have a subscription to BioMed Central. The Libraries are hosting the online archive of locally published journals with back issues (three titles to date)."

"The library has dedicated financial resources to build a scholarly publishing office which publishes OA journals. Although the journals still take on the cost of acquisition, review and editing, our office provides electronic content preparation services and hosting free of charge to them."

"The library runs an OJS service that currently hosts two titles, and hopes to expand. So we have costs associated with providing the service. We also pay a yearly fee to BioMed Central to facilitate publication by local authors. I believe this is the only case in which the library directly subsidizes author fees."

"We are members of BioMed Central, Public Library of Science. We support Stanford Encyclopedia of Philosophy, and similar. We pay author's fees for IOP. In addition, there is some in-kind contribution as we process and host local content."

"We fund author fess and offer support for certain Open Access packages/titles out of our Collections Budget."

"We host one journal on our server and we are members of Public Library of Science and are investigating membership in BioMed Central."

"We host two journals now and expect to add more through our digital imprint, Newfound Press. We currently subscribe to Public Library of Science, and previously, to BioMed Central. We have also contributed to the Stanford Encyclopedia of Philosophy project."

CATALOGING

9. If the library includes catalog records for OA resources in the OPAC, how are the records obtained or created? Check all that apply. N=65

	N	Locally Hosted N=45	Externally Hosted N=64
Download records from OCLC	55	19	55
Library staff create original, full records	52	39	44
Acquire records from another third party such as Serials Solutions	37	3	36
Library staff create original, brief records	35	25	22
Acquire records from other libraries (e.g., consortial partners)	21	1	21
Other method	11	5	7

Please specify other method.

Selected Comments from Respondents

Locally Hosted

"Automated harvesting of XML metadata."

"Faculty create their own records."

"For ETDs, MARC records will be exported from our repository workflow management system."

"Metadata created for image management system (Greenstone; Luna Insight)."

"Some contributors to IR provide metadata."

Externally Hosted

"Automated harvesting of XML metadata."

"ERM creates brief records."

"Generated from ERM."

"Government documents records are also supplied to us via MARCIVE."

"OCLC LTS catalogues monographs."

"Provided by vendor (e.g., ProQuest)."

"Publisher provided."

"We generally add a link to the OA resource to a pre-existing record for the print version of the resource; we occasionally download records from RLIN."

10. If library staff create catalog records for OA resources, are they the same staff who create catalog records for other electronic resources? N=63

Yes	60	95%
No	3	5%

Please briefly describe which staff create catalog records for OA resources (e.g., title(s) or categories of staff, number of professional and support staff.) Approximately how much time is spent each month cataloging OA resources?

Staff Category	Amount of Time Spent Cataloging
1 cataloging librarian	Unknown
1 Electronic Resources Cataloger (Professional) 1 Serials Cataloger (Professional) 2 Paraprofessional Catalogers	16 Hours
1 Electronic Resources Cataloguer – librarian 4 Library Assistants (level 4) Support staff	Varies, between 5 and 10 hours
1 professional 2 support staff	8–10%
1 professional librarian	We don't track the amount of time spent on this.
2 librarians 2 staff	NA
2 support staff	40 hours/month
2 support staff in serials cataloging	30 hours
3 cataloguing librarians	As required
3 professional catalogers 1 staff member	100 hours/month
5 Library Specialists (paraprofessionals)	2 hours
A recent reorganization has increased the number of staff dedicated to cataloging of all e-resources, including OA. We now have 2 librarians and 3 support staff	
In ERMS, paraprofessionals as part of ERMS maintenance. Records from ERMS also are OpenURL and OPAC records. In IR: Teaching/research faculty and student assistants; professional librarian, student staff with professional review.	Less than 20 hours per month by library personnel
All of these staff work with OA materials as needed. None is assigned full time. Cataloging and serials department personnel, assigned based on assigned subject/format areas. Cataloging: 6 professional, 12, paraprofessional. Serials: 3 paraprofessionals.	Variable, but not too much.
Both professional and technical staff in Acquisitions and Bibliographic Access divisions plus dedicated cataloging staff in several special collections	Unknown
Catalogers and electronic resource staff 3 professional 5 support	4 hrs
Cataloging staff	20
Cataloguing librarians	NA

Staff Category	Amount of Time Spent Cataloging
Cataloguing support staff, but majority of records are automatically generated by our ERM.	3 hours
Copy-based catalogers in serials & monograph cataloging units (8)	NA
Different library units have their own approaches; some units have professionals assigning metadata, others have support staff and some have both levels of staff.	No way to know. Very minor portion of catalog work— probably less than 1% of total time spend on cataloging.
Either professional or support staff. Largest type of materials is theses and dissertations which are primarily handled by support staff.	2 hours
Electronic Resources Cataloger 1 professional	Very little - less than 1% of cataloger's monthly time
Faculty and paraprofessional catalogers create catalog records, both within our METS-based Workflow Management System and through OCLC for direct export to the SIRSI Unicorn OPAC.	5%
For individually cataloged items, Electronic resource specialists in the cataloging department provide cataloging. For batches of harvested items, library systems staff provide the load services and configuration.	10–20 hours for individually cataloged items. Less for batch loaded materials.
For OA resources for which cataloguing copy is readily available (e.g., books from National Academy Press, Canadian government documents), any one of a group of clerical staff may handle these. Most of the work on OA journals is done by a higher level of staff with BAs (similar to library technicians, but with all library training in-house) using copy from other libraries. For OA resources that have no copy elsewhere, such as the 2 journals hosted locally (because they were brand new), a professional librarian (me!) creates the records.	Less than 2 hours
Head of Cataloging [faculty librarian] Serials Cataloging Supervisor [exempt staff supervisor]	Almost none
Librarian catalogers.	4 hrs
Librarians 5 support staff (LAIII-LAV)	We don't track. Cataloging open access is part and parcel of the normal workload.
Library Assistants (paraprofessionals) in Acquisitions and Rapid Cataloging unit (4 total)	Unable to estimate
Library assistants who may have some library techniques courses, or who are trained on the job; they are not professional catalogers.	NA

Staff Category	Amount of Time Spent Cataloging
Library Associates	5 hours
Library IV (upper level staff member) registers OA journals with Serials Solutions in addition to cataloging other e-resources. Librarian III (professional librarian) creates K-level cataloging for locally hosted resources.	2–3 hours
Library Sp. Sr. 1 Library Specialist 2-4 Catalog Librarians	5 hours
Library technical assistants (3) Professional (1)	NA
Main Library:	We do not keep track of the amount of staff times spent on cataloging only OA resources.
Monograph and Serials Catalogers and cataloging support staff	NA
Monographic catalogers catalog OA books; serials catalogers catalog OA serials, etc.	
One full time serials librarian (as a component of her responsibilities for managing serials cataloging), with occasional support from 1.5 FTE original catalogers (as needed)	2–5 hours
1 original cataloging librarian handles these materials as a part of regular workflow.	1–2 hours
1 professional librarian 3 support staff	Unknown (insignificant amount <5 hrs/month)
Selected limited records are cataloged by one professional staff and one support staff	5 to 15 hours
Serials Cataloger (professional)	Less than 2 hours
Serials catalogers	A miniscule amount
Serials catalogers (librarians and non)	Up to 120 hrs depending on volume of state docs and ETDs
Serials catalogers both paraprofessional and professional, this is a tiny part of the job of several individuals.	Unknown. About 10 titles per month are added to the catalog.
Technical services faculty and staff.	Unknown
Technical Services staff	NA
The records are created by Cataloging and Serials staff. It is done primarily through the use of MARCit! and coverage loads in III.	5 hours

Staff Category	Amount of Time Spent Cataloging
The UCLA Library Cataloging and Metadata Center consists of 15 FTE librarians and 29 FTE staff. Copy cataloging for e-resources is done by staff ranked at Library Assistant III and above; original cataloging for e-resources is done by staff ranked at a Library Assistant V or above (Librarian).	Unable to quantify at the present time.
This work is done by two Cataloging and Metadata Services Librarians (professionals) and one Cataloging and Metadata Services Specialist II (senior support staff).	2 hours
Three categories of staff: high level support staff (10) Professional assistants (2) Library faculty (5)	25–30 hours per month
Three full-time professionals and two full-time paraprofessionals in the AUL Cataloging Department create catalog records for OA resources.	No more than 2 hours per month
We do not treat these resources any differently from non-OA resources; cataloguing staff would integrate this into their workload.	Unable to determine

11. If catalog records are created, are they contributed to OCLC? N=63

Yes	56	89%
No	7	11%

12. If the library includes links to OA resources in catalog records, are the resources identified by some kind of field or tag (e.g., a local series entry)? N=65

Yes	26	40%
No	39	60%

If yes, please briefly describe how they are labeled.

Selected Comments from Respondents

"039 Marc tag."

"856 field - URL source"

"856 field indicator is 40"

"856 PURL"

"856 subfield z = freely available online."

"856 tag 1 labeled as "linked resource.""

"856 tag subfield z Free"

"Added entry for package or 'Open Access resource selected by the UCSD Libraries ...'"

"Coded as 'free web' but not distinguished from other free or 'free with print' resources."

"DOAJ titles have a 730 'Directory of open access journals.'"

"Either in the 856 $z or by the nature of the persistent URL assigned to the resource."

"Either with an added author (usually corporate) entry, or an added title or series entry."

"For theses and dissertations there is a computer file tag. There is no particular tag to indicate OA."

"Labeled in a corporate entry field: [Name of Resource]- York University."

"Locally created series statements."

"May not be specified as OA. Electronic Resources have note: Web site/Electronic Resource – URL. Also have holding record with location listed as: Electronic Resource."

"Most open access journals include a 730 of 'Open access journals.' Additionally, open access journals do not include a note regarding access restrictions (845) whereas licensed resources do include this note in the OPAC record."

"Note field and holdings record indicate this."

"Our local projects are identified by a series statement, external resources tend to not be so identified."

"Records from the California Digital Library Shared Cataloging Program include a title hook in the 793 field 'Open Access Resource; Selected by the UC Libraries.' Other open access resources are not identified in any field or tag, but are recognizable by the absence of any note specifying restrictions on access, e.g., 'Restricted to UCI' or 'Restricted to UC Campuses.'"

"SFX button or 856 link."

"The subfield z in the 856 identifies the source (Government web site, Federal Reserve Bank of Minneapolis, etc.) It does not specifically identify that this source is open access."

"There is no special labeling. Full catalog records are contributed to OCLC, brief catalog records are not."

"URLs are added to holding records. Notes include: Freely accessible; Free access made available at the publishers discretion."

"Various fixed and variable length fields depending on the nature of the record."

"We use the MARC 773 field to identify open-access resources."

LINK MAINTENANCE

13. How does the library monitor changes and/or maintain links to externally hosted OA resources? Check all that apply. N=67

Respond to reports of problems	60	90%
Rely on data provider (e.g., Serial Solutions) for link checking	43	64%
Link checking software or scripts from a third-party, please specify	22	33%
Do not systematically monitor or maintain links locally	19	28%
Link checking software or scripts that are locally developed	14	21%
Other method, please describe	8	12%

Selected Comments from Respondents

"Circulation students systematically review links."

"For GPO PURL, rely on GPO."

"Link checking software from ILS."

"Local shareware programs."

"Manual checking."

"MarcIt records/updates from SFX."

"Student manual link-checking."

"We use the ILS linking software to identify and correct broken links."

Link checking software:

Innovative Interfaces checkbot (2 responses)

Innovative Interfaces URL Checker module

JTurl

LinkBot (2)

LinkScan

OCLC PURL link checker software (3)

Voyageur LIS software

WebLinkValidater

Xenu (3)

Link checking software provided by the university

Software provided by library ILS

"Currently investigating new software."

14. Has the library experienced any other significant link maintenance issues that are unique to OA resources? N=64

Yes	8	12%
No	56	88%

If yes, please briefly describe the problem and how the library addressed it.

Selected Comments from Respondents

"3000+ OA journals in link resolver have frequent URL changes and require more maintenance than average title. Also have tendency to disappear."

"In local Electronic Resources database the links are checked infrequently. Links break and it is difficult to trace to correct resource. Manually checked in ERDB, now moving to Serials Solutions, they do most work. Occasionally, we find a problem and send it to them. Not as time consuming as before."

"Not significant problems, but it is our impression that URLs may change more frequently than other resources or journals may go from open access to subscription-based without notification."

"OA resources are no more volatile than the paid titles; equally problematic for maintenance."

"OA resources, particularly Canadian government documents, seem to be less stable than our subscribed resources. The government documents are the group most likely to have URL changes that we are not notified about except through problem reports."

"Occasionally, there are titles that are listed as OA but are not full OA or are not OA at all. Those problems we fix in our SFX Knowledgebase and report problems to SFX."

"Often it takes longer for OA sites to resolve technical difficulties at their end. Normally if a free e-resource is not available we delete it. We tend to give truly OA sites a little longer before making this decision."

"Sometimes a title seems to be free and then it requires payment. Sometimes a title drops from DOAJ because it no longer meets their criteria and we point to DOAJ in our link resolver."

"These 'free' e-journals often move to paid subscriptions without notifying libraries, and in some instances they vanish without notice."

"Unstable links; URL changes. Links are repaired or removed."

"Web sites are often down, URLS change, items/titles are no longer available (titles 'go away)."

"We've found that link maintenance issues are not unique to OA resources."

USAGE TRACKING

15. Does the library track the usage of OA resources? N=67

	N	Locally Hosted N=54	Externally Hosted N=66
Yes	41	25	36
No	39	29	30

If yes, please briefly describe the tracking method.

Selected Comments from Respondents

Locally Hosted Only

"All locally owned OA resources are stored in the repository. Downloads are tracked for statistical purposes. RULs for open source journals are treated hierarchically as collections (title level), subcollections (issue level), and objects (article level)."

"COUNTER plugin that is bundled with the Open Journal Systems software tracks full text access by month. Statistics module bundled with DSpace tracks bitstream views, item views, IPs, searches performed, etc."

"Statistics package in institutional repository software."

"Use of local holdings may be gaged through analysis of server logs."

"We collect data for each resource on: the number of sessions, number and types of searches, number and types of browses, and number of views."

Externally Hosted Only

"Data, when available from the publisher (OA or otherwise) is centrally compiled and reviewed by subject selectors."

"If in SFX, yes we track usage via SFX, otherwise no."

"In theory, if in SFX KB, can get usage statistics and if tracking from A&I (or other source) databases can get usage stats."

"NetTracker Number of ClicksStats from SFX and Metalib."

"Only when vendor provided usage statistics are available."

"Our open-URL resolver (SFX) provides indirect usage data."

"SFX statistics."

"Statistics from open URL resolver."

"Through the usages statistics in Serials Solutions."

"Usage statistics from publisher."

"Usage can be tracked via the library's electronic resource a-z list or via SFX."

"Usage of externally hosted OA journals & databases are tracked in the same ways that non-OA titles are tracked. Locally developed E-metrics Tracking Tool & publisher stats are retrieved."

"Usage statistics are available through our link resolver."

"Vendor-supplied statistics."

"We can get usage stats from SFX for the free resources."

"Web gateway statistics."

Both Locally and Externally Hosted

"Externally hosted: if the title is offered by a vendor or publisher that supplies usage data, we can track usage. Locally hosted: library Web usage statistics are collected locally."

"For local: 123LogAnalyzer. For external: vendor reports and Serials Solutions click-through statistics."

"In our institutional repository, we have recently installed counters (etds, LOs). We do keep SFX data and from time to time use extract reports. In the case of BioMed Central only we download the stats from the publisher. With digitized Web pages we can track page hits but haven't done much of this to date."

"Internal URL resolver."

"Internal: Net Tracker software; External: Serials Solutions."

"It depends on the source—some usage statistics are pulled from our own databases and other statistics are supplied to us from third parties or from our consortium."

"Local index counter."

"Local programming was created to track use."

"Local stats come from our internal usage logs. External stats, unless provided by the supplier, which is rare in the case of OA titles, come primarily from our SFX and Proxy logs."

"Locally and externally hosted resources are tracked by local logging procedures, analysis of SFX transaction database, and vendor supplied stats in the case of the IR."

"Locally hosted: Web hits for these products, internal statistics using the OJS software. Externally hosted:

usage stats from the vendor."

"Locally hosted: server logs and repository software. Externally hosted: report from SFX of statistics for collections of OA journals in the SFX knowledgebase."

"Locally hosted: tracked on Web page by internal counter. Externally hosted: tracked by in-house internal counter."

"Locally hosted: we have usage statistics for documents in our institutional repository. Externally hosted: we have usage statistics for some OA titles in our link resolver (SFX), for examples titles in the DOAJ (Directory of Open Access Journals) list."

"Locally: local Web server usage stats. Externally: primarily Ser.Solutions for journals."

"Statistics are gathered via the SFX Linkresolver for those in SFX. DSpace software used for the Research Exchange provides usage statistics."

"Usage reporting built into system."

"We track OA titles locally in the same manner that we track other resources through our home grown Electronic Resources Web interface; however, we do not distinguish OA from other online resources."

"We track usage of our online resources if possible. We use statistics from publishers whenever possible, and also collect 'click through' statistics for our electronic journals. For OA monograph publications, we have little or no tracking of usage."

"Web logs, Serials Solutions reports, in some cases usage logs in COUNTER format from open access sites that provide this."

PROMOTING USE OF OA RESOURCES

16. Please indicate what methods the library has used to help library staff and users understand what open access is and to alert library users to the availability of OA resources. Check all that apply. N=56

Include OA resources in pathfinders or subject guides	44	79%
Discuss OA resources during instruction sessions	30	54%
Discuss OA resources in newsletter articles	27	48%
Library Web page that explains what OA resources are	26	46%
Discuss OA resources during the reference interview	25	45%
Send e-mail alerts about newly available OA resources	20	36%
Other method, please describe	20	36%

Selected Comments from Respondents

"793 is visible to patrons."

"A 'globe' icon identifies Open Access resources on our Index & Database list."

"Campus forums."

"Contact faculty."

"Discuss in meeting with faculty groups."

"ERM gateway indicates OA resources in note."

"Faculty discussion/presentations, University Committees."

"Faculty office visits."

"Faculty presentations; information in our IR brochure; using SPARC brochures."

"Held a forum in 2005 on OA publishing."

"In preparation: invitational session for OA contributors; campus-wide: survey of OA awareness and participation."

"In the course of collection assessment reports to faculty have identified OA resources and as a result have added them to OPAC or Web pages."

"Meetings with faculty groups; distribution to all faculty of ACRL/ARL open access flyer."

"Open access is a major topic in current discussions with faculty and with the Council on Libraries."

"Provide special search functionality in the library's Web site to search only free and open access materials. Meet with faculty to discuss open access alternatives for publication. Discuss during departmental meetings issues surrounding economics of publishing and open access. DOAJ, PubMed Central, and BioMed Central journals are cataloged separately and identifiable via our local OPAC."

"RSS feeds generated from catalog."

"Some OA information is included in the Scholarly Communication Web pages."

"We treat OA resources like other resources."

"Web site designed to advocate open access issues."

"Worked with university to establish campus OA fund to support publishing fees."

17. Does the library promote OA resources any differently than other electronic resources? N=67

Yes	17	25%
No	50	75%

If yes, please briefly explain the difference.

Selected Comments from Respondents

"For OA documents in our institutional repository, our Digital Initiatives staff notify the library of new electronic theses and dissertations, new collections of other documents, or updates in the number of items available."

"Generally, we would not, but as this is something new to researchers, we have a larger awareness campaign to undertake. Researchers have questions about author fees, etc. which we need to explain. Promotion then focuses on some of the unique issues with OA resources and why the library supports these resources."

"Highlight in newsletters."

"In larger context of scholarly communication issues."

"In sense that we promote in communications with faculty and grad students about scholarly communication issues; we don't promote differently in terms of resource usage."

"Locally digitized collections (state docs and cultural heritage materials) promoted through conference presentations, press releases, posters, etc."

"OA resources get much less attention when it comes to marketing. We are having a hard time reaching our patrons with the promotion of paid resources. We just have not put much effort into promoting OA resources."

"Resources that are paid for tend to get higher level of 'press.'"

"There tends to be less emphasis on OA resources than on purchased e-resources. OA is of lower priority to promote as a whole. However, if a valuable resource in a field of study happened to be OA, there would be no hesitancy in promoting and providing access."

"These are targeted for examples of changes in Scholarly Communication model."

"We have a robust Scholarly Communications outreach program. The promotion of OA resources and publishing alternatives is key to our Scholarly Communication education plan."

"We do promote our institutional repository more aggressively than other OA resources."

"We have a Web page that indicates discounts available to faculty to support publication in author pays type open access resources. As part of our promotion of UC eScholarship, we discuss opportunities for establishing new open-access journals with faculty who are interested."

"We have promoted DOAJ and PLos as scholarly publishing models for the common good of the academic community and models with high potential for sustainability."

"We promote our online journal application—a modification of the open source OJS system—as a service provided by the libraries' repository."

"We tend to more heavily promote resources for which the library has paid."

"Yes, they are featured in campus-wide newsletters."

ADDITIONAL COMMENTS

18. Please enter any additional information regarding open access resources at your library that may assist the author in accurately analyzing the results of this survey.

Selected Comments from Respondents

"Local consortium is producing shared catalogue records for provincial open access government publications."

"OA titles fully integrated into our e-resources policies & procedures. We support alternative titles in our subject areas, e.g., by purchase of relevant SPARC titles."

"Open access resources are fully integrated into library selection and processing practices, and library discovery tools. Library bibliographers are communicating with faculty about open access issues and opportunities. Bibliographers' Annual Reports include a Scholarly Communication section: 'Describe any faculty involvement in open access publishing initiatives.' Inclusion of this section helps promote and record results of conversations on this topic, and identify specific resources where appropriate to the subject area."

"Open access resources are not treated any differently than any other resources we wish to promote. We always try to match the appropriate resource to the need our patron expresses. If the need can be fulfilled by the use of an open access resource, the resource will be included in the recommendations."

"Use and promotion of use of open access resources varies by subject area selector and bibliographer. Some staff actively seek out these resources and ask for them to be cataloged. Some selectors never do."

"We don't have a collection policy for OA materials. If a resource is identified in a subject area relevant to the university, we add it like any paid resource. We are just beginning an institutional repository though we do have some cool local resources available through the library."

"We found several of these questions difficult to answer, since we don't really think of OA titles as different from anything else. They are woven into our overall selection and access mechanisms is such a way that makes it difficult to tease out minor differences in approach."

"We have a vast collection of e-material. We have challenge enough with cataloging all parts of our 'paid for' resources. Consequently, the shifting sands of OA get less treatment. On the other hand, OhioLINK and Serials Solutions allow us to track major portions of the OA journal collections through tools that are heavily used locally."

"We have created a small OA repository of local reports, pre-prints and other documents, but they are not yet widely available via OAI."

"We host journals using Open Journal Systems and conference proceedings using Open Conference Systems."

"While we are happy to take advantage of OA resources by linking to them once they've been identified as valuable, we have rarely made any push to add them to our resources (an exception would be BioMed Central; we have tried to add all its journals, and the free backfiles from HighWire Press). Our efforts have been focused mainly on paid resources and there has never been time to do much to seek out OA resources."

RESPONDING INSTITUTIONS

University at Albany, SUNY

University of Alberta

Arizona State University

Auburn University

Boston College

Brigham Young University

University of British Columbia

University of California, Davis

University of California, Irvine

University of California, Los Angeles

University of California, San Diego

University of California, Santa Barbara

Case Western Reserve University

University of Chicago

University of Cincinnati

Colorado State University

University of Connecticut

Dartmouth College

Duke University

Florida State University

University of Georgia

Georgia Institute of Technology

University of Guelph

University of Hawaii at Manoa

University of Illinois at Urbana-Champaign

Indiana University Bloomington

University of Iowa

Iowa State University

Johns Hopkins University

Kent State University

University of Kentucky

Library of Congress

Louisiana State University

University of Louisville

McMaster University

University of Manitoba

University of Massachusetts, Amherst

Massachusetts Institute of Technology

University of Miami

University of Michigan

University of Minnesota

University of Missouri-Columbia

Université de Montréal

University of Nebraska-Lincoln

University of North Carolina at Chapel Hill

North Carolina State University

Northwestern University

University of Notre Dame

Ohio State University

University of Oklahoma

Oklahoma State University

University of Pennsylvania

Pennsylvania State University

University of Pittsburgh

Rice University

Rutgers University

Smithsonian Institution

University of Southern California

Southern Illinois University Carbondale

Syracuse University

Temple University

University of Tennessee

University of Utah

University of Virginia

Virginia Tech

Washington State University

University of Waterloo

Wayne State University

University of Western Ontario

Yale University

York University

REPRESENTATIVE DOCUMENTS

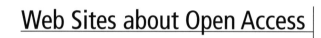

Web Sites about Open Access

http://library.albany.edu/divs/digital/oa.html

UNIVERSITY LIBRARIES
UNIVERSITY AT ALBANY State University of New York

Need Help?   Search this Site   Site Index

Open Access

Open Access is a term widely used to describe refereed scholarly communication available online that is not restricted by copyright nor by price barriers. See below for a more detailed definition

Peter Suber, editor of the highly popular Open Access News blog and the SPARC Open Access Newsletter, has produced an excellent, extensive list of practical steps people can take to move Open Access forwards. Whether you are a faculty member, a librarian, student, a society, funder or government body, Suber provides many suggestions for positive contributions you can make to the Open Access movement today:

What You Can Do To Promote Open Access
http://www.earlham.edu/%7Epeters/fos/do.htm

General resources:

Articles and Papers on Open Access by the Association of Research Libraries
http://www.arl.org/info/publicaccess/Leg/articles.html

Open Access [Public Library of Science]
http://www.plos.org/about/openaccess.html

Budapest Open Access Initiative
http://www.soros.org/openaccess/

Open Access Bibliography by Charles Bailey
http://info.lib.uh.edu/cwb/oab.pdf

The Open Archives Initiative
http://www.openarchives.org/

Open Access Materials Available on the World Wide Web:

Open Access Archives and Repositories
http://www.earlham.edu/%7Epeters/fos/lists.htm#archives

Jan Szczepanski's list of Open Acess Journals
http://www.his.se/templates/vanligwebbsida1.aspx?id=20709

Definition of Open Access from the Public Library of Science:

An Open Access Publication [1] is one that meets the following two conditions:

1. The author(s) and copyright holder(s) grant(s) to all users a free, irrevocable, worldwide, perpetual right of access to, and a license to copy, use, distribute, transmit and display the work publicly and to make and distribute derivative works, in any digital medium for any responsible purpose, subject to proper attribution of authorship, [2] as well as the right to make small numbers of printed copies for their personal use.
2. A complete version of the work and all supplemental materials, including a copy of the permission as stated above, in a suitable standard electronic format is deposited immediately upon initial publication in at least one online repository that is supported by an academic institution, scholarly society, government agency, or other well-established organization that seeks to enable open access, unrestricted distribution, interoperability, and long-term archiving (for the biomedical sciences, PubMed Central is such a repository).

[1] Open access is a property of individual works, not necessarily journals or publishers.

Other scholarly communication links:

2005 New NIH Public Access Policy Resources

Scholarly Communication Issues and Resources

News About Scholarly Communication

OA / UofA Home | UofA Libraries Home

OA / UofA

Open Access Publishing Information for the University of Alberta Community

ABOUT OPEN ACCESS

- What is Open Access
- OA Browsing & Searching
- UA Research Visibility
- UA News
- UA Organizations
- UA Conferences
- UA Reading List
- Open University OA Support
- UofA Scholarly Publishing Resources
- Help & Contact Us

UNIVERSITY OF ALBERTA
LIBRARIES

SEARCH

  (Search)

UofA Libraries OA Support

We, at the University of Alberta Libraries, are committed to the principles of Open Access (OA), as outlined in the UofA Statement on Open Access Scholarly Literature and Research Information Content. Open Access benefits researchers and learners by equalizing access to research information and facilitating scholarly communication. The University of Alberta Libraries include OA products in our collections, and provide support for members of the University of Alberta community who want to publish in OA formats. For more information about Open Access, please contact your subject librarian.

The University of Alberta Libraries supports many Open Access publishing initiatives:

SPARC (Scholarly Publishing and Academic Resources Coalition)
The UofA Libraries support SPARC as a first supporter, which includes an institutional membership agreement for journals which are SPARC publishing partners. Our SPARC open access commitments are:

- **BioMed Central**
  The University of Alberta Library's supporter membership with BMC reduces the author publication fee by 50% for UofA authors. View a list of recent articles published by UofA authors.

- **Public Library of Science**
  The UofA Library's institutional membership entitles UofA authors to a 10% reduction in the publication fee. View a list of recent articles published by UofA authors.

- **List of UA sponsors of each journal**

Open Content Alliance (OCA)
The OCA represents the collaborative efforts of a group of organizations from around the world that will help build a permanent archive of multilingual digitized text and multimedia content.

UNIVERSITY OF CALIFORNIA

http://osc.universityofcalifornia.edu/

Reshaping **Scholarly Communication**

💠 Publisher and Journal Profiles   💠 Model Copyright Clauses

UNIVERSITY of CALIFORNIA
Office of Scholarly Communication

Search | Site Map

Regain Control of Scholarly Communication

The University of California's scholars and their partners across the academy are reshaping scholarly communication. Understand the challenges, the crises they have produced, and opportunities to address them.
View a summary...

There are publishing alternatives that are faster, more flexible and less costly than commercial journals.

Ben Crow · Professor of Sociology, UC Santa Cruz

Current News & Issues

· Survey of UC Faculty attitudes & behavior
· Reviews of proposed UC Open Access Policy
· Other recent UC-related news

The Facts

Current scholarly publishing models are not economically sustainable. Researchers and students have access to a diminishing fraction of relevant scholarship. But remedies and alternatives are being developed and tested. Learn about:

· The economics of publishing
· Alternatives for scholarly communication

UC Responses

· eScholarship Publishing Initiatives
· Systemwide Faculty Committee
· Systemwide Administrative Committee
· UC Libraries' Program
· Office of Scholarly Communication

TAKE ACTION

Scholars, influence the scholarly communication system to increase the impact and benefit of your scholarship.

💠 **Review and discuss the UC Open Access Policy proposal**

💠 **Manage your intellectual property**
· Retain certain copyrights
· Maximize the reach and impact of your work

💠 **Use alternative forms of publishing**
· Deposit your work in open access repositories
· Submit to open access journals

💠 **Support sustainable scholarly communication**
· Wield your influence with publishers
· Promulgate society publishing best practices
· Support publishing experiments and new business models

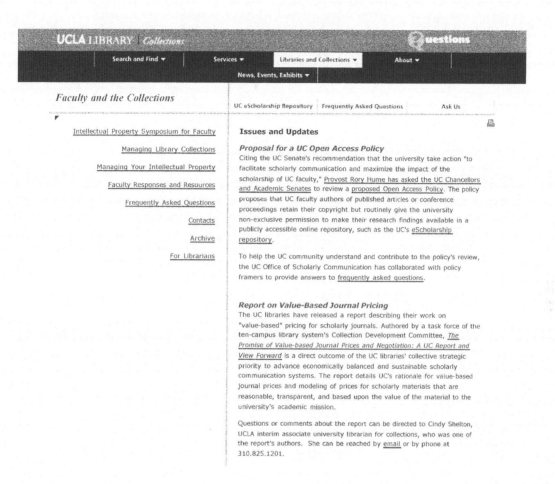

UCLA LIBRARY | *Collections*   **Q**uestions

| Search and Find ▼ | Services ▼ | Libraries and Collections ▼ | About ▼ |

News, Events, Exhibits ▼

Faculty and the Collections

UC eScholarship Repository   Frequently Asked Questions   Ask Us

Intellectual Property Symposium for Faculty

Managing Library Collections

Managing Your Intellectual Property

Faculty Responses and Resources

Frequently Asked Questions

Contacts

Archive

For Librarians

Issues and Updates

Proposal for a UC Open Access Policy
Citing the UC Senate's recommendation that the university take action "to facilitate scholarly communication and maximize the impact of the scholarship of UC faculty," Provost Rory Hume has asked the UC Chancellors and Academic Senates to review a proposed Open Access Policy. The policy proposes that UC faculty authors of published articles or conference proceedings retain their copyright but routinely give the university non-exclusive permission to make their research findings available in a publicly accessible online repository, such as the UC's eScholarship repository.

To help the UC community understand and contribute to the policy's review, the UC Office of Scholarly Communication has collaborated with policy framers to provide answers to frequently asked questions.

Report on Value-Based Journal Pricing
The UC libraries have released a report describing their work on "value-based" pricing for scholarly journals. Authored by a task force of the ten-campus library system's Collection Development Committee, *The Promise of Value-based Journal Prices and Negotiation: A UC Report and View Forward* is a direct outcome of the UC libraries' collective strategic priority to advance economically balanced and sustainable scholarly communication systems. The report details UC's rationale for value-based journal prices and modeling of prices for scholarly materials that are reasonable, transparent, and based upon the value of the material to the university's academic mission.

Questions or comments about the report can be directed to Cindy Shelton, UCLA interim associate university librarian for collections, who was one of the report's authors. She can be reached by email or by phone at 310.825.1201.

Updated: Sunday, September 16, 2007 12:21
Privacy Policy | User Rights and Responsibilities | Contact the Web Administrator | Giving to the Library

http://www.libs.uga.edu/science/research.html

home » science library » open access movement

Open Access Movement

The UGA Libraries support the Open Access movement. Rising journal prices coupled with decreasing budgets necessitate changes in publishing methods. The Open Access movement leads the way in providing research in a timely fashion at minimal charge, allowing for quick dissemination of important research findings. The scientific community in particular has led the way in providing up-to-date scholarly research in the Open Access environment.

Background Information About the Open Access Movement:

Create Change is an organization dedicated to promoting the equitable dissemination of scholarly research.

OpenDOAR is an authoritative directory of academic open access repositories. As well as simply listing repositories, OpenDOAR provides tools and support to both repository administrators and service providers in sharing best practice and providing tools to improve the quality of the repository infrastructure.

SPARC is the Scholarly Publishing and Academic Resources Coalition formed through the Association of Research Libraries as a way to address the escalating prices of journals.

Washington DC Principles for Free Access to Science movement is led by publishers in the science and medical fields.

Open Access Publishers Specific to the Scientific Community:

AGRICOLA is a bibliographic database of citations to the agricultural literature created by the National Agricultural Library.

AgZines: "a harvest of free agricultural journals."

BioOne indexes articles in the Bioscience arena.

The Directory of Open Access Journals provides a listing of journals that participate in the Open Access Movement. The journals are arranged both alphabetically and topically.

Free Medical Journals provides a listing of over 1300 freely available journals in the medical field.

HighWire Press hosts the largest on-line repository of life science, peer-reviewed articles from high profile journals.

The International Network for the Availability of Scientific Publications offers a listing of freely available on-line journals

The Open Directory Project provides a listing of freely available journals on the Worldwide Web.

Lehigh University's list of resources pertaining to the Open Access movement.

The Public Library of Science contains Open Access works in the biological sciences on "all aspects of biology from molecules to ecosystems".

Science Library

About Us
Books of the Month
Contact Us
Current Display
Directions
Endnote / Refworks
Hours
Interlibrary Loan
Request Research Help
Science Directory
Suggest a Purchase

http://www.library.gatech.edu/scholarlycommunication/response.htm

 **Georgia Tech** | **Library and Information Center**

INFORMATION ABOUT: | OPEN ACCESS AND SCHOLARLY COMMUNICATION | NEWS:

CRISIS IN SCHOLARLY COMMUNICATION

THE COLLECTIVE RESPONSE

THE GEORGIA TECH RESPONSE

• Serials Review website
• Open Access @ GT

RESOURCES:

• for Authors
• for Librarians

The Collective Response

What is being done?

One response to the scholarly communication crisis is the Open Access (OA) Movement. In its purest form, Open Access publishing provides immediate, free public access to scholarly publications on the Internet, whether in the form of open access journals or through some form of archiving. What makes it possible is the Internet and the consent of the author or copyright-holder. For the past several years, open access publishing initiatives have been proposed to increase the visibility of scholarly output. See Peter Suber's **Open Access Overview** for an historical perspective and more information about the initiative.

OA is entirely compatible with peer review, and all the major OA initiatives for scientific and scholarly literature insist on its importance. Just as authors of journal articles donate their labor, so do most journal editors and referees participating in peer review. OA literature is not free to produce, even if it is less expensive to produce than conventionally published literature. The importance is not a cost-less system, but a better way to make research available with as few barriers to this information as possible.

Self-Archiving
Institutional Repositories
Disciplinary Repositories

Open Access Publishing
OA Journals
OA Publishers
OA Directories

Self-Archiving

▸ Institutional repositories:

Institutional repositories capture the digital-born intellectual output of an academic institution in support of its teaching and research missions. For more information about Georgia Tech's IR visit **SMARTech** (Scholarly Materials and Research at Tech).

Examples of content typically ingested in IRs include:

Annual Reports, Computers Programs, Conference Papers, Data Sets, Learning/Complex Objects, Models, Pre-Prints/Post-Prints, Proceedings, Research Reports, Simulations, Technical Reports, Web Pages, White Papers and Working Papers

Examples:
California Digital Library eScholarship
CalTech CODA
Cornell Dspace Open Access Repository
DigitalCommons @ Johns Hopkins University
Georgia Tech SMARTech
MIT DSpace
NCSU Faculty Publications Repository
Purdue E-Scholar
ScholarlyCommons@Penn
Texas A&M TxSpace
University of Illinois Urbana-Champagne IDEALS
University of Michigan Deep Blue
University of Tenn Knoxville Scholars archive repository
University of Texas Digital Repository
University of Washington Dspace
University of Wisconsin MINDS@UW

▸ Disciplinary repositories

Examples:

arXiv.org (Physics)

NEWS:

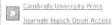 Latest SPARC Open Access Newsletter

 Cambridge University Press Journals launch Open Access

Provosts from nearly 50 universities support public access legislation

http://www.library.gatech.edu/scholarlycommunication/response.htm

Open Access Publishing

> Open Access Journals:

Journal of International Commercial Law and Technology, published
by the International Association of IT Lawyers (IAITL)
Carbon Balance and Management, published by BioMed Central
Electronic Journal of Geotechnical Engineering, published by World
Wide Web of Geotechnical Engineers
Electronic Journal of Boundary Elements, published by Scholarly
Communication Center, Rutgers University
Journal of Educational Technology & Society, published by IEEE
Computer Society
Digital Journal of Opthalmology, Massachussetts Eye and Ear
Infirmary, a teaching affiliate of Harvard Medical School
IETF Journal (Internet Engineering Task Force), published by the
Internet Society
Information Technologies and International Development (ITID),
published by MIT Press

Library-hosted Open Access Journals:

Southern Spaces, Digital Library Research Initiative, Robert W. Woodruff
Library, Emory University
Journal of Cognitive Affective Learning, Digital Library Research
Initiative, Robert W. Woodruff Library, Emory University
CTheory Multimedia, published by Cornell University Library

> Open Access Publishers:

PLoS
Pub Med Central
Bio Med Central

> Open Access Directories:

ROAR (Registry of Open Access Repositories)
OpenDOAR (Directory of Open Access Repositories)
DOAJ (Directory of Open Access Journals)
SPARC: List of Institutional Repositories
SPARC EUROPE: Institutional Repository Initiatives in Europe
NDLTD (Networked Digital Library of Theses and Dissertations)

ACCESSIBILITY | CONTACT US | LEGAL & PRIVACY INFORMATION | TECHNOLOGY
©2005 Georgia Institute of Technology :: Atlanta, Georgia 30332

JOHNS HOPKINS

Scholarly Communications Group ● Knowledge Without Barriers

The Johns Hopkins Scholarly Communications group is dedicated to fostering open access to quality information in support of learning, scholarship, research and patient care.

The group promotes

● increasing awareness among scholars, administrators and policy makers of the importance of retaining certain rights over their intellectual property

● initiatives and practices that encourage competition in the publishing of scholarly information and supports practices which facilitate free exchange of scholarly information

 NIH Policy FAQ

Scholarly Communication at Risk

- The Issues
- The Facts
- A Call to Action

Now Available:
Ownership &
Access in Scholarly
Publishing Forum
Archive

Click for Details

Author's Tools

Organizations & Institutions

NEW Publishing Models

Readings

Contact Us

About Us

[Search]

News & Events

09-18-07 SciVee: YouTube for Scientists
09-12-07 Open Access to Scientific Memoirs
09-11-07 Elsevier Makes Oncology Articles Free

more news on events

http://info-libraries.mit.edu/scholarly/open-access-initiatives/

Scholarly Publication - MIT Libraries
Retaining rights & increasing the impact of research

Open Access Initiatives

Open Access: What is It?

"Open Access" defines a movement that promotes free, unrestricted Internet access to the primary research literature as a public good. Definition of the concept emerged from three conferences:

- Berlin Declaration on Open Access to Knowledge in the Sciences and Humanities
- Bethesda Statement on Open Access Publishing
- Budapest Open Access Initiative

Also see: An Overview of Open Access

Open Access Policies from Major Research Funders:

- NIH Public Access Policy
- HHMI Public Access Publishing Policy
- Federal Research Public Access Act
- Open Access Mandates in the UK, Europe, and Canada
- Summaries of Research Funders' Open Access Policies

NIH Public Access Policy

The original National Institutes of Health proposal in September 2004 attempted to balance Open Access to NIH-funded research results with economic and business needs, by asking NIH principal investigators to deposit their peer-reviewed articles in PubMed Central (the NIH's digital repository for biomedical research) following a six month waiting period. The final proposal, announced on February 3rd, 2005, requests deposit "as soon as possible", within twelve months of publication.

- Original NIH Notice: Enhanced Public Access to NIH Research Information
- AAU Statement on NIH Public Access Proposal [pdf]
- NAS endorsement of "Enhanced Public Access to NIH Research Information"
- Taxpayers Support "Open Access" to NIH Research

- Final NIH policy
- NIH Manuscript Submission System (Implementation of NIH Policy)
- NIH FAQ about manuscript submission

Howard Hughes Medical Institute [HHMI] Public Access Publishing Policy

The HHMI announced on June 26, 2007 that it will "require its scientists to publish their original research articles in scientific journals that allow the articles and supplementary materials to be made freely accessible in a public repository within six months of publication."

The policy applies to all manuscripts submitted by HHMI scientists on or after January 1, 2008.

More details.

Federal Research Public Access Act of 2006

FRPAA is a bipartisan effort to increase tax payers' access to federally funded research. The Act would require that manuscripts of journal articles stemming from grants made by US government agencies funding more than $100 million in research annually be available openly on the internet — without payment or subscription barriers — within six months of publication elsewhere in a peer-reviewed journal. This legislation was introduced on May 2, 2006 by Senators John Cornyn (R-TX) and Joe Lieberman (D-CT).

The Act would also require that the manuscripts be preserved in a digital archive maintained by the funding agency, or in another suitable repository that permits free public access, interoperability, and long-term preservation.

Eleven government agencies would be affected: The Departments of Agriculture, Commerce, Defense, Education, Energy, Health & Human Services, Homeland Security, and Transportation, as well as the Environmental Protection Agency, the National Aeronautics and Space Administration, and the National Science Foundation. (Only nonclassified research is covered by the Act.)

FRPAA is consistent with existing copyright and patent laws; the funding agency would need to obtain a non-exclusive right to disseminate manuscripts resulting from their grant funds. Researchers accepting funding from these agencies would need to avoid transferring exclusive rights to publishers of their journal articles, to allow for public dissemination in accordance with this Act.

In February 2007, *Wired News* reported the first public confirmation that Senator Cornyn plans to re-introduce FRPAA in the current session of Congress.

For more information on FRPAA:

http://info-libraries.mit.edu/scholarly/open-access-initiatives/

- Official wording of the bill and FAQ
- SPARC's summary
- Colorado State University Libraries' Newsletter article
- Peter Suber's Summary/Analysis

Open Access Mandates in the UK, Europe, and Canada

Wellcome Trust (UK)

The Wellcome Trust, an independent charity that funds research to improve human and animal health, is the largest private funder of medical research in the UK. In October, 2005, it became first research funding agency in the world to require open access to all publications resulting from its grants.

The Wellcome Trust position statement in support of open and unrestricted access to published research requires that "any research papers that have been accepted for publication in a peer-reviewed journal, and are supported in whole or in part by Wellcome Trust funding, to be deposited into PubMed Central (PMC) or UK PMC once established, to be made freely available as soon as possible and in any event within six months of the journal publisher's official date of final publication."

The policy is also significant in its clear statement that an author's obligations to the Wellcome Trust pre-date and take precedence over "any agreement with a journal." Papers submitted for publication on or after October 1, 2006 must be submitted to journals that have a Wellcome Trust compliant publishing policy.

The position statement also includes an expectation that "authors...where possible... retain their copyright" and guarantees funding to cover page processing charges authors may face when working with publishers who support the open access model.

Research Councils (UK)

As of September 2007, 6 of the 7 Research Councils in the UK had adopted open access mandates. These councils provide a significant portion of publicly funded research in the UK. Sample open access mandates include:

- Biotechnology & Biological Sciences Research Council (BBSCR)
- Economic & Social Research Council (ESRC)
- Medical Research Council (MRC)
- Natural Environment Research Council (NERC)

European Commission:

In the largest government allocation to OA infrastructure in history, the European Commission has budgeted roughly 50 million pounds for the period 2007-08.

In addition, the following European research funding organizations are among those which have established Open Access mandates or recommendations:

- European Research Council
- France: Inserm (Institut national de la santé et de la recherche medicale) – OA required from 2008
- Germany: Deutsche Forschungsgemeinschaft (DFG)

Canada:

- The Canadian Institutes of Health Research (CIHR) announced a new open access policy that takes effect January 1, 2008. It requires those receiving grant funds from CIHR to "make every effort to ensure" their research articles are made freely available within six months of publication.

Summaries of Research Funders' Open Access Policies:

- Research funders: Sherpa's Juliet database
- Research funders and University OA Policies: ROARMAP
- Funders of biomedical research: OA policies: from BioMed Central

More information

- FAQ
- Podcasts on Scholarly Publishing & Copyright
- Recent commentary on open access and scholarly publishing
- Dispelling Myths about Open Access
- More on Open Access Initiatives
- Open Access and Scholarly Monographs
- MIT Impacts

http://www.hsl.unc.edu/Collections/ScholCom/index.cfm

Open Access & Scholarly Communications

The Health Sciences Library supports Open Access, Open Archives, and Open Repositories as methods to encourage the widest possible access to scholarly content.

Open Access
Scholarly content made available free of charge to anyone upon publication

Open Archives
Scholarly content in subscription publications made available free of charge after an initial embargo period.

Open Repositories
Digital collections of scholarly content on a particular subject or the collected intellectual works of an institution or group of institutions.

Sign the Petition for Public Access to Publicly Funded Research in the United States.

If you are a researcher whose work is funded by the federal government, your signature is especially important since it shows that you want your work to be shared and used.

The Alliance for Taxpayer Access

What You Can Do

#1 Keep Your Copyrights

- Contact Deborah Gerhardt, UNC Copyright and Scholarly Communications Director
- UNC Journal Author's Agreement
- Copyright Resources for Authors (SPARC)

#2 Publish in Open Access Journals

- Funding Supports Open Access Fees
  - Get Application for UNC-CH Funding
- BioMed Central
  Our institutional membership, effective until Feb 2008, covers article processing fees for UNC-Chapel Hill authors.
- Public Library of Science
  Our institutional membership currently covers 15% of UNC-Chapel Hill author's fees.
- Directory of Open Access Journals

#3 Deposit Your Work in a Repository

- PubMed Central
  Author Manuscripts and NIH Public Access Policy
- OpenDoar
  Provides a quality-assured listing of open access repositories around the world.

UNC Activities

- Publishing Choices: Know Your Rights and Expand Your Impact. With Heather Joseph, Executive Director of SPARC. View video of Heather Joseph's presentation at UNC, April 2007.
- Reading the Fine Print. Chronicle article by UNC's Deborah Gerhardt on negotiating publication contracts.
- Organizing the World's Organization: Google's Vision for the 21st Century. View video of Craig Silverstein's presentation at UNC, October 2006.
- UNC-CH Authored Articles in Open Access Journals (PubMed search)
- Scholarly Communications in a Digital World: A Convocation (January 27-28, 2005)
- UNC-Chapel Hill Scholarly Communications Working Group
- CRADLe - Center for Research and Development of Digital Libraries

About Open Access

- Open Access (Create Change)
- Open Access - A Primer (Funk)
- 2005 Survey of Journal Author Behavior (Rowlands & Nicholas)
- "Impact Factor" Revisited (Dong, Loh & Mondry)

Learn More

- Six things that researchers need to know about open access (Suber)
- Open Access News Blog (Suber)
- Open Access Citation Impact Bibliography (OpCit Project)
- Scholarly Electronic Publishing Bibliography (Bailey)

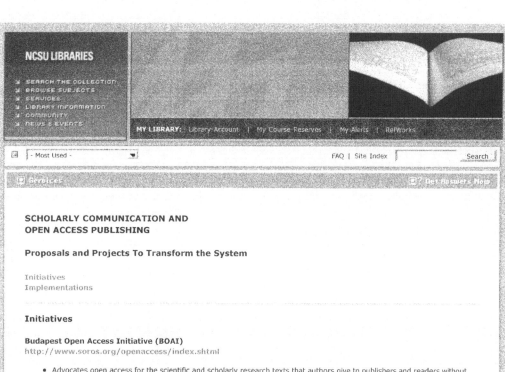

**SCHOLARLY COMMUNICATION AND
OPEN ACCESS PUBLISHING**

Proposals and Projects To Transform the System

Initiatives
Implementations

Initiatives

Budapest Open Access Initiative (BOAI)
http://www.soros.org/openaccess/index.shtml

- Advocates open access for the scientific and scholarly research texts that authors give to publishers and readers without asking for any kind of royalty of payment
- Only concerns access to future research literature
- Focus is on peer-reviewed research literature
- Author consent (relinquishing payment, not intellectual property rights, i.e., not placing in the public domain)

BOAI defines "open access" as the free availability on the public internet, permitting any users to read, download, copy, distribute, print, search, or link to the full texts of these articles, crawl them for indexing, pass them as data to software, or use them for any other lawful purpose, without financial , legal, or technical barriers other than those inseparable from gaining access to the internet itself. The only constraint on reproduction and distribution, and the only role for copyright in this domain, should be to give authors control over the integrity of their work and the right to be properly acknowledged and cited.

Scholarly Publishing and Academic Resources Coalition (SPARC)
http://www.arl.org/sparc/

- SPARC®, is an alliance of universities, research libraries, and organizations built as a constructive response to market dysfunctions in the scholarly communication system. SPARC serves as a catalyst for action, helping to create systems that expand information dissemination and use in a networked digital environment while responding to the needs of academe.
- Goal is to foster competition in scientific communication by facilitating cost-conscious, high-quality journals to compete head-to-head with existing high-cost journals.
- SPARC Open Access Newsletter
  http://www.arl.org/sparc/soa/index.html

Public Library of Science (PloS)
http://www.plos.org/

- A nonprofit organization of scientists "committed to making the world's scientific and medical research freely accessible to scientists and the public around the world."
- Goal to open the doors to the world's library of scientific knowledge by giving any scientist, physician, patient, or student - anywhere in the world - unlimited access to the latest scientific research.
- Publishes several open access journals. All works are open access, i.e., immediately available without cost to anyone to use subject only to the condition that the original authorship is properly attributed. Copyright is retained by the author.

- Publications fees (payable by author, institution, or funding agency) are $1500 per article; discounts are available with institutional memberships.

Washington D.C. Principles For Free Access to Science
A Statement from Not-for-Profit Publishers
http://www.dcprinciples.org/statement.htm

The **DC Principles** outlines the commitment of not-for-profit publishers to work in partnership with scholarly communities such as libraries to "ensure that these communities are sustained, science is advanced, research meets the highest standards and patient care is enhanced with accurate and timely information." The **DC Principles** provide what has been called the needed "middle ground" in the increasingly heated debate between those who advocate immediate unfettered online access to medical and scientific research findings and advocates of the current journal publishing system.

[return to top]

Implementations

"Open Access" Models

PubMed Central (PMC) (http://www.pubmedcentral.nih.gov/)

- The U.S. National Library of Medicine's digital archive of life sciences journal literature
- An e-print initiative providing free, unrestricted online access to the full text of life science research articles
- Not a journal publisher
- Copyright remains with the journal or author

BioMed Central (BMC) (http://www.biomedcentral.com)

- 50 online, peer reviewed journals in biology and medicine Independent, commercial publishing house
- Free access
- Authors retain copyright
- Funded by author fees or institutional membership
- Pricing model: base article processing charge of $525 per article multiplied by the number of articles published by authors affiliated with an institution in BioMed Journals during the previous 12 months
- TRLN Letter to BioMed Central (http://www.trln.org/BioMed Central letter.pdf)

Public Library of Science (PloS) (http://www.plos.org)

- Not just an initiative (see above); publishes several highly regarded open access journals
- Treats cost of publishing as the final integral step in the funding of a research project

Public Access to NIH-Funded Research

The National Institutes of Health (NIH) is now promoting open access to research it funds. For research funded by NIH; electronic versions of all scholarly publications resulting from the research must be deposited into PubMed as soon as possible, but no later than 12 months after official publication. This policy is weaker than the original proposal that called for deposit in six months, it is a step in the right direction.

National Institutes of Health, "Policy on Enhancing Public Access to Archived Publications Resulting from NIH-Funded Research"

More information on public access from the NIH

[return to top]

"Cost-Effective" Subscription Access Models

BioOne (http://www.bioone.org)

- Biological, ecological, and environmental science journals
- Full text offered
- Small societies and non-commercial publishers
- American Institute of Biological Sciences, SPARC, University of Kansas, Greater Western Library Alliance & Allen Press

Highwire Press (http://highwire.stanford.edu)

- Division of the Stanford University Libraries
- Online versions of high-impact, peer-reviewed journals (355) with a focus on STM
- Hosts largest repository of free full-text life sciences articles in the world (some parts of Highwire are free; others are not or provide delayed access)
- Available through institutional and individual subscriptions

Repositories

Repositories containing scholarly output are included in the open access movement, along with open access journals. Models of institution- and discipline-based content have been developed.

[return to top]

http://library.osu.edu/sites/sel/chem/Open_Access.php

University Libraries ◘ Science and Engineering Library

OSUL Home · Find · Borrow · About OSUL · Libraries · Learn · Off-campus Sign-in · My Record · Help

Science & Engineering Library
September 26, 2007

175 West 18th Avenue
Columbus, Ohio 43210
(614) - 292 - 0211

SEL

SEL Homepage

Library Services

Hours and Info

Floor Guide

Getting to Ackerman Library

Newsletters

Staff

Blog

New Books at SEL

SEL Displays

Mission Statement

Gifts & Donations

Digital Union

Tips

Handouts for Resources

Identify Articles & Locate Journals

Find Theses

Use your Laptop

Decode Citations

Cite Resources

Read Call Numbers

Check This

BBC Science & Nature

Open Access: A Primer

What is Open Access?

Open access journals are journals that use a funding model that does not charge readers or their institutions for access.

What is a repository?

A repository is a place where scholars can deposit digital content they have created. These open access repositories accept all types of scholarly materials, including pre-publication materials, journals and peer-reviewed series, seminar series papers, post-prints, and more. Repositories ensure the dissemination and preservation of that content in way that a departmental or faculty website cannot.

University of California's e-Scholarship Repository

The Ohio State University's Knowledge Bank.

Where can I find open access journal titles?

- Full Text Journals in Chemistry

- Directory of Open Access Journals

- Public Library of Science
  - PLoS Biology
  - PLoS Computational Biology
  - PLoS Genetics
  - PLoS Medicine
  - PLoS Pathogens

- BIOMED Central
  - Immunome Research
  - Journal of Ethnobiology and Ethnomedicine
  - Biological Knowledge
  - Biology Direct
  - Diagnostic Pathology
  - International Breastfeeding Journal
  - Journal of Biomedical Discovery and Collaboration
  - Philosophy, Ethics, and Humanities in Medicine
  - Substance Abuse Treatment, Prevention, and Policy
  - Synthetic and Systems Biology

- American Society for Biochemistry and Molecular Biology (ASBMB)
  - Journal of Biological Chemistry

CNN Science & Space

Science News

Science Daily

- Journal of Lipid Research
- Molecular & Cellular Proteomics

- Institute for Condensed Matter Physics of the National Academy of Sciences of Ukraine
    - Condensed Matter Physics

- Libertas Academica
    - Cancer Informatics
    - Evolutionary Bioinformatics Online (EBO)

- The Japan Society of Histochemistry and Cytochemistry
    - Journal of Histochemistry & Cytochemistry
    - Acta Histochemica et Cytochemica

- National Institute of Standards and Technology
    - Journal of Physical & Chemical Reference Data Fulltext v1-27 (1972-1998) [free]

- Library Publishing Media
    - Journal of RNAi and Gene Silencing

- The Federation of European Biochemical Societies
    - European Journal of Biochemistry Fulltext v1-271 (1967-2004) 12 month moving wall
    - FEBS Journal (Fulltext v272+ (2005+) 12 month moving wall) review articles only

- Science Direct
    - FEBS Letters (Fulltext v1+ (1968+) 12 month moving wall)

Please send any comments or suggestions to: SEL Page Master

http://www.lib.utk.edu/colldev/issues.htm

Scholarly Communications Issues

Scholarly communications involve complex dynamics among intellectual property, the economics of publishing, technological developments, legislative action, and the academic culture for research, publication, promotion, and tenure. A number of factors, especially the increasing commercialization of scholarly publishing and dramatic increases in journal costs, have decreased scholars' access to essential research resources all over the world. Each year fewer scholarly publications are available to scholars worldwide. Universities are acquiring a smaller portion of available journals and monographs, even though the production of scholarly information is growing exponentially. Faculty members publish articles that universities buy back at premium prices.

Administrators, scholars and librarians are pursuing options for "reclaiming" the research produced in the academy. National information associations, scholarly societies, librarians, and researchers are experimenting with alternatives to make scholarly research easily accessible to scholars, their students, and to the world at large. Their efforts are resulting in the emergence of systems for collecting and disseminating peer-reviewed articles online and growth in personal web sites that contain faculty publications. Libraries are becoming scholarly publishers. Universities are creating digital repositories of the intellectual work of their faculty and students. The following links connect to associations, projects, and visions illustrative of sharing scholarly communications for the common good.

UT Scholarly Communications Committee

UT Blog: Scholarly Communication Issues @ the UT Libraries

Associations
Association of Research Libraries Office of Scholarly Communications
Council on Library and Information Resources
Digital Library Federation

Raising Awareness
Changing Scholarly Publishing: A Guide for Graduate Students (brochure)
Scholars Under Siege: Changing our Scholarly Publishing Culture (brochure)
ARL Brochures
The Book & the Scholar: Celebrating the Year of the University Press
Talking Points for Discussions with Faculty and Graduate Students
University of Tennessee Faculty Senate Scholarly Publishing Resolution, May 1, 2006
Cornell University Library Issues in Scholarly Communication
Scholarly Communication: Academic Values and Sustainable Models (UC Berkeley Center for Studies in Higher Education)
Libraries & Scholarly Communication (University of California Libraries)
Off the Page and Onto the Web...Essays on Scholarly Publishing @ UT
Scholarly Communications (Boston College Libraries)
Scholarly Publishing & The Common Good: Changing our Culture (University of Tennessee symposium)

Intellectual Property
Copyright Information for University of Tennessee Faculty
University of Tennessee Office of the General Counsel
Know Your Copyrights (Association of Research Libraries)New!
Creative Commons Licenses
University of Minnesota Copyright Information and Education
The University of Texas Office of the General Counsel
North Carolina State University Scholarly Communication Center

Open Access
Framing the Issue: Open Access
Budapest Open Access Initiative
Directory of Open Access Journals
Open Access News (Blog edited by Peter Suber)

Tools for Open Access Publishing
BOAI Open Access Journal Guides
Open Journal Systems (free software for journal management and publishing)

http://www.lib.wayne.edu/geninfo/about/scholarly_communications/

RESOURCES   FOR FACULTY
SERVICES   FOR STUDENTS
LIBRARY INFO

Scholarly Communications at WSU

The current model of scholarly communication is not sustainable. Libraries and their parent institutions are unable to support the increasing volume and rising costs of scholarly resources. As a result, libraries have no choice but to cancel some journal subscriptions and reduce book purchases as well. The causes of this are many and the solutions are complex. The Libraries at WSU have taken several steps ensure that our clients continue to have access to the resources they need.

How are the WSU Libraries responding to the rising cost of journals?

How are the WSU Libraries facilitating use of open access journals?

How are the WSU Libraries supporting open access publishing?

How are the WSU Libraries preserving access to scholarly literature?

How are the libraries preserving access to WSU's intellectual and cultural output?

Suggestions | Privacy | Acceptable Use

http://www.library.yale.edu/science/oa.html

Yale University Science Libraries

Research Tools / Services / Beginning Research / About the Libraries

Open Access Journals: an overview

This page points to a variety of resources to help explain and update the status of the Open Access journal initiative.

Our definition of open access is: freely available immediate access to published peer reviewed research articles.

The Open Access journal initiative offers a new model for supporting peer review and distribution of scholarly information. The basic plan is to provide free access to published peer-reviewed research articles. This may be immediate access, or articles may be available only after an embargo period. The embargo is often placed by the publisher in order to guarantee subscriptions revenue to cover infrastructure costs (peer review coordination, editing, archiving, etc.)

An alternative to subscription revenue is the introduction of direct or indirect author page charges. A number of granting agencies are now supporting or encouraging the use of grant funds to provide immediate Open Access articles. This author or institutional article fee model is being explored and it is too soon to determine if such a pricing model will be viable on a large scale. For libraries, a model in which annual fees are based upon unpredictable annual production is rather difficult to budget.

There are a number of sites that provide information about this controversial topic:

1. Yale Science Libraries' OA news page,
2. Yale Libraries' Future of Scholarly Publishing Forum site,
3. Forum: Scholarly Publishing Resources list

4. OA description page (Director's opinion page),
5. Open Access: User benefits and concerns (Director's presentation outline)

Other resources about Open Access may found as links on our Yale SciLib Possible Journal Cost Solutions and Enhancements page.

Comments

Search / Contact Us / Yale University Library / Yale University / YaleInfo

Updated: 07/23/07
Maintained by: Davel Stern
© 2005 Yale University

QUICK LINKS

RESEARCH TOOLS
Orbis Library Catalog
Online Databases
Online Journals
Help Getting Started

SERVICES
Ask a Reference Question, and IM
Renew Books
View Your Library Account
Request Items in Yale Libraries
Borrow Direct
Interlibrary Loan
Book Purchase Request
View Course Reserves
Reserve Book Request Form

SCIENCE LIBRARIES & COLLECTIONS
General Science
Astronomy
Biology
Chemistry
Computer Science
Engineering
FES
Geology
Mathematics
Medicine
Physics

Science Libraries Home
Hours
Paper Journal Comments
News

Newsletter Articles and Blogs

http://scholcommbc.blogspot.com/

SEARCH BLOG   FLAG BLOG   Next Blog»   Create Blog | Sign In

BOSTON COLLEGE | UNIVERSITY LIBRARIES
SCHOLARLY COMMUNICATION NEWS@BC
PROVIDING UP-TO-DATE NEWS ON THE RAPIDLY CHANGING SCHOLARLY COMMUNICATION LANDSCAPE

FRIDAY, SEPTEMBER 21, 2007

Boston Library Consortium Partners with Open Content Alliance

On 20 September, 2007 the **Boston Library Consortium** announced that it was partnering with the **Open Content Alliance** to provide open access to a large number of digitized books.

From the **Press Release**

> The Boston Library Consortium, Inc. (BLC) announced today that it will partner with the **Open Content Alliance** to build a freely accessible library of digital materials from all 19 member institutions. The BLC is the first large-scale consortium to embark on such a self-funded digitization project with the Open Content Alliance. The BLC's digitization efforts will be based in a new scanning center, the Northeast Regional Scanning Center, unveiled today at the Boston Public Library.
>
> The Consortium will offer high-resolution, downloadable, reusable files of public domain materials. Using Internet Archive technology, books from all 19 libraries will be scanned at a cost of just 10 cents per page. Collectively, the BLC member libraries provide access to over 34 million volumes.
>
> The BLC's Executive Director, Barbara G. Preece commented "The Boston Library Consortium is excited about its partnership with the Open Content Alliance and its members. The Consortium believes that this collaboration is the living articulation of the BLC's view to expand access to its rich resources held by the membership. The BLC/OCA project will ensure that materials digitized will remain free and open to scholars and the public."

Full Text of **Press Release**

POSTED BY BRENDAN RAPPLE AT 2:48 PM   0 COMMENTS

WEDNESDAY, SEPTEMBER 19, 2007

Publishers' PR Tactic Angers University Presses and Open-Access Advocates

On Tuesday, 11 September, 2007 we posted a letter from Heather Joseph, Executive Director of SPARC, about PRISM – the Partnership for Research Integrity in Science and Medicine" **http://www.prismcoalition.org**. PRISM is an anti-open access initiative launched with development support from the Association of American Publishers that specifically targets efforts to expand public access to federally funded research results - including the National Institute of Health's Public Access Policy. In the 21 September issue of *The Chronicle of Higher Education* Jennifer Howard provides an update on the consternation caused by PRISM's anti-open access efforts.

Extracts from The Chronicle Article

> The Association of American Publishers has landed in hot water with university presses and research librarians, as well as open-access advocates, thanks to a new undertaking that is billed as an attempt to "safeguard the scientific and medical peer-review process and educate the public about the risks of proposed government interference with the scholarly communication process." . . . .
>
> Reactions to Prism have been widespread and vigorous, with some commentators calling for a **boycott** of the association. The news provoked one university-press director, Mike Rossner of Rockefeller University Press, to make a public **request** that a

---

ABOUT

Scholarly Communication News@BC provides information updates for the Boston College community about developing scholarly communication issues, policy debates, legislation and innovative examples of dissemination/discourse practices, and is managed by staff of the **Boston College Libraries**. The Library welcomes contributors for both posting and commenting. If you are interested in posting please contact Brendan Rapple or Mark Caprio. Comments will be reviewed by blog moderators with respect to blog purpose and scope.

RELATED LIBRARY PAGES

BC's Suggested Addendum to Publishing Contracts
eScholarship@BC Repository: An Overview
Publishing Trends & Research Libraries

RECOMMENDED SITES

Alliance for Taxpayer Access
Boston Library Consortium, Authors' Rights and Publishing
Budapest Open Access Initiative
Create Change: A Resource for Faculty and Librarian Action to Reclaim Scholarly Communication
Open Access News (Blog by Peter Suber)
Scholarly Publishing and Academic Resources Coalition (SPARC)
SHERPA: Opening Access to Research

ACADEMIC SCHOLARLY COMMUNICATION BLOGS

Duke University
Georgia State University
University of Illinois at Urbana-Champaign
University of Minnesota

BLOG ARCHIVE

▼ 2007 (126)

　▼ September (8)

　　Boston Library Consortium Partners with Open Conte...
　　Publishers' PR Tactic Angers University Presses an...
　　Carlyle Letters Online: Magnificent New Open Acces...
　　Usage of Open Content Licences by Cultural Organis...
　　SPARC letter to members on the PRISM anti-open acc...
　　Open Access to Health Research Publications: CIHR ...
　　Faculty Attitudes and Behaviors Regarding Scholarl...
　　Latest SPARC Open Access Newsletter

　► August (2)
　► July (13)
　► June (19)
　► May (18)

disclaimer be placed on the Prism Web site "indicating that the views presented on the site do not necessarily represent those of all members of the AAP." Mr. Rossner continued, "We at the Rockefeller University Press strongly disagree with the spin that has been placed on the issue of open access by Prism."

The Association of Research Libraries sent its members a **talking-points memo**, dated September 4, that deals with some of the arguments made on the Prism site. The librarians' group wrote that Prism "repeatedly conflates policies regarding access to federally funded research with hypothesized dire consequences ultimately resulting in the loss of any effective system of scholarly publishing. Many commentators agree that inaccuracies abound in the initiative's rhetoric." . . . .

Brian D. Crawford, chairman of the executive council of the AAP's professional and scholarly publishing division, acknowledged that the strength of the negative reaction had taken his group by surprise. "We did not expect to have encountered the sort of criticism that we have seen thus far," Mr. Crawford told *The Chronicle*. "We were truly hoping to establish this as a way to have a very productive dialogue on what are important and nuanced issues." . . . .

Mr. Crawford defended his group against charges that it is anti-open access. "We're definitely not saying that open access equals faulty science," he said. "What we're saying is, It's important for publishers to have the flexibility to introduce and experiment with whatever business model they wish to, without government intervention."

Because of the criticisms, however, the publishers' group is taking "under advisement" the idea of adding a disclaimer, as Mr. Rossner suggested. It's also possible that the association will decide to revise the language on the Prism Web site in response to the concerns of university presses and libraries. . . . .

Full Text of The Chronicle Article

POSTED BY BRENDAN RAPPLE AT 3:16 PM 0 COMMENTS

FRIDAY, SEPTEMBER 14, 2007

Carlyle Letters Online: Magnificent New Open Access Resource

Duke University Press has just launched the **Carlyle Letters Online** on HighWire Press. This database/web site is freely available to institutions and individuals.

From the press release:

> Duke University Press announces the launch at **http://carlyleletters.org/** of the Carlyle Letters Online: A Victorian Cultural Reference, the electronic edition of The Collected Letters of Thomas and Jane Welsh Carlyle.
>
> A fully digitized version of one of the most comprehensive literary archives of the nineteenth century, the Carlyle Letters Online features thousands of letters written by Scottish author and historian Thomas Carlyle (1795 - 1881) and his wife, Jane Welsh Carlyle (1801 - 1866), to over six hundred recipients throughout the world.
>
> In part because of grants from the National Endowment for the Humanities and the Delmas Foundation, the Carlyle Letters Online is currently available at no charge to institutions and individuals.
>
> Undertaken in partnership with HighWire Press, a division of Stanford University Libraries, the Carlyle Letters Online is one of the first electronic scholarly editions to

BOSTON COLLEGE

http://scholcommbc.blogspot.com/

be published by a university press. Leveraging HighWire's award-winning online hosting platform and suite of features, the collection offers users an unprecedented level of functionality and personalization.

Designed as a 'collection that knows itself,' each letter in the collection is comprehensively indexed and searchable by date, subject, and recipient, with similar letters linked to each other through a vast web of interconnectivity that encourages discovery and facilitates research. Users may also take advantage of a simple and free registration to employ an array of personalized features, including saved searches; access to a 'My Carlyle Folder,' in which users can create a personal archive; and options for managing personal alerts to find out when the site is updated.

Created for scholars of all levels, from high school students to professionals, the collection allows users to explore the Victorian era from the unique vantage point of two people placed squarely at the geographic, political, and intellectual center of their century. While a critical reference for Victorian scholars, the Carlyle Letters Online aims also to encourage interdisciplinary study, appealing not just to students of literature and history but also to those of politics, economic history, and women's studies.

For more information about the Carlyle Letters Online, including coordinating editor Brent E. Kinser's introduction to the Carlyles, the history of the print edition, and the history of the electronic project, please visit **http://carlyleletters.org/**

POSTED BY BRENDAN RAPPLE AT 3:34 PM   0 COMMENTS

WEDNESDAY, SEPTEMBER 12, 2007

Usage of Open Content Licences by Cultural Organisations in the UK

The **Eduserv foundation** has funded a **study** looking into usage of open content licencing by cultural organisations in the UK.

Jordan Hatcher, formerly a Research Associate at the AHRC Research Centre for studies in Intellectual Property and Technology Law, is leading a study into how open content licences are currently being used by cultural organisations in the UK. The study began in June, 2007 and is being funded by the Eduserv Foundation. Ed Barker of Eduserv is assisting with the work.

Digital resources produced by publicly funded organisations are a valuable asset to the research and education community. Many people in the sector believe that access to and use of these digital resources could be better and that the wider use of open content licences would help to improve the situation.

A study titled "The Common Information Environment and Creative Commons" was funded by Becta, the British Library, DfES, JISC and the MLA on behalf of the Common Information Environment. The work was carried out by Intrallect and the AHRC Research Centre for studies in Intellectual Property and Technology Law and a report was produced in the Autumn of 2005. During the Common Information Environment study it was noted that there was considerable enthusiasm for the use of Creative Commons licences from both cultural heritage organisations and the educational and research community. In this study we aim to investigate if this enthusiasm is still strong and whether a significant number of cultural heritage organisations are publishing digital resources under open content licences.

For more detailed information about this study, please refer to the **full proposal**.

POSTED BY MARK CAPRIO AT 6:30 AM   0 COMMENTS

TUESDAY, SEPTEMBER 11, 2007

SPARC letter to members on the PRISM anti-open access effort

Heather Joseph, SPARC Executive Director, has issued a **letter** to SPARC members about "PRISM" an anti-open access lobbying initiative.

Extracts (**Full letter here**):

Dear SPARC Members

I'm writing to bring to your attention the recent launch of an anti-open access lobbying effort. The initiative, called 'PRISM – the Partnership for Research Integrity in Science and Medicine' (**http://www.prismcoalition.org**), was launched with development support from the Association of American Publishers and specifically targets efforts to expand public access to federally funded research results – including the National Institute of Health's Public Access Policy.

The messaging on the PRISM Web site which is aimed at key policy makers, directly corresponds to the PR campaign reportedly undertaken by the AAP earlier this year. As Nature reported in January, AAP publishers met with PR "pit bull" Eric Dezenhall to develop a campaign against the "free-information movement" that focuses on simple messages, such as "public access equals government censorship," and suggested that "the publishers should attempt to equate traditional publishing models with peer review".

This campaign is clearly focused on the preservation of the status quo in scholarly publishing, (along with the attendant revenues), and not on ensuring that scientific research results are distributed and used as widely as possible. The launch of this initiative provides a timely opportunity for engaging faculty members, researchers, students and administrators in dialogue on important issues in scholarly communications.

To assist in this conversation, the Association of Research Libraries has prepared a series of talking points that explicitly address each of the PRISM messages listed above. These very useful talking points can be found at **http://www.arl.org/bm~doc/issue-brief-aap-pr-prism.pdf**

The reaction to the launch of PRISM by the academic research community has been immediate and quite strong. . . .

PRISM developments will be of interest to many on campus – including those who follow open access and anyone who is involved with PRISM publishers as an author, editor, or subscriber. Please feel free to share this information. To stay abreast of related news, visit the SPARC Web site (**http://www.arl.org/sparc**) or Peter Suber's Open Access News blog (**http://www.earlham.edu/%7Epeters/fos/fosblog.html**).

If you have any comments or questions about this discussion, please don't hesitate to contact me through (202) 296-2296 or email heather@arl.org.

Warm regards,

Heather Joseph

POSTED BY BRENDAN RAPPLE AT 7:22 PM 0 COMMENTS

FRIDAY, SEPTEMBER 7, 2007

Open Access to Health Research Publications: CIHR Unveils New Policy

The Canadian Institutes of Health Research (CIHR) recently announced a new policy to promote public access to the results of research it has funded. CIHR will require its researchers to ensure that their original research articles are freely available online within six months of publication.

From the **Press Release**:

> Under this new Policy, which will apply to all grants awarded after January 1, 2008 that receive funding in whole or in part from CIHR, grant recipients must make every effort to ensure that their peer-reviewed research articles are freely available as soon as possible after publication. This can be achieved by depositing the article in an archive, such as PubMed Central or an institutional repository, and/or by publishing results in an open access journal. A growing number of journals already meet these requirements and CIHR-funded researchers are encouraged to consider publishing in these journals.

> Additionally, grant recipients are now required to deposit bioinformatics, atomic, and molecular coordinate data, as already required by most journals, into the appropriate public database immediately upon publication of research results.

From the official **policy on Access to CIHR-funded Research Outputs**:

5.1.1 Peer-reviewed Journal Publications

- Grant recipients are now required to make every effort to ensure that their peer-reviewed publications are freely accessible through the Publisher's website (Option #1) or an online repository as soon as possible and in any event within six months of publication (Option #2).

- Under the second option, grant recipients must archive the final peer-reviewed full-text manuscripts immediately upon publication in a digital archive, such as PubMed

http://scholcommbc.blogspot.com/

accessible within six months of publication, where allowable and in accordance with publisher policies. Grant recipients may use the **SHERPA/RoMEO database** to locate summaries of publisher copyright policies. The SHERPA/RoMEO database will help grant recipients determine which journals allow authors to retain copyright and/or allow authors to archive journal publications in accordance with funding agency policies. However, CIHR recommends confirming with editorial staff whether archiving the postprint immediately, and making it freely accessible within six months, is permissible.

POSTED BY BRENDAN RAPPLE AT 3:41 PM   0 COMMENTS

MONDAY, SEPTEMBER 3, 2007

Faculty Attitudes and Behaviors Regarding Scholarly Communication: Survey Findings from the University Of California

The Office of Scholarly Communication, University of California recently released a report **"Faculty Attitudes and Behaviors Regarding Scholarly Communication: Survey Findings from the University Of California."** This report is an analysis of over 1,100 survey responses covering a range of scholarly communication issues from faculty in all disciplines and all tenure-track ranks.

Full Report, 124 pages [download PDF]
Executive Summary and Summary of Findings, 10 pages [download PDF]
Survey Instrument, 10 pages [download PDF]

Results From the Executive Summary:

* Faculty are strongly interested in issues related to scholarly communication.
* Faculty generally conform to conventional behavior in scholarly publication, albeit with significant beachheads on several fronts.
* Faculty attitudes are changing on a number of fronts, with a few signs of imminent change in behaviors.
* The current tenure and promotion system impedes changes in faculty behavior.
* On important issues in scholarly communication, faculty attitudes vary inconsistently by rank, except in general depth of knowledge and on issues related to tenure and promotion.
* Faculty tend to see scholarly communication problems as affecting others, but not themselves.
* The disconnect between attitude and behavior is acute with regard to copyright.
* University policies mandating change are likely to stir intense debate.
* Scholars are aware of alternative forms of dissemination but are concerned about preserving their current publishing outlet.
* Scholars are concerned that changes might undermine the quality of scholarship.
* Outreach on scholarly communication issues and services has not yet reached the majority of faculty.
* The Arts and Humanities disciplines may be the most fertile disciplines for University sponsored initiatives in scholarly communication.
* Senior faculty may be the most fertile targets for innovation in scholarly communication.

POSTED BY BRENDAN RAPPLE AT 5:41 PM   0 COMMENTS

Older Posts

Subscribe to Posts (Atom)

http://www.lib.uci.edu/libraries/update/spring05/spring05.html

Volume 23, Number 3, Spring 2005

UCI Libraries Update

A Newsletter for Faculty

1 2 3 4 5 6 7 8 9 Next »

Message from the University Librarian:
Open-Access for Scholarly Communication

The UCI Libraries provide faculty with options for submitting articles to peer reviewed, open-access digital journals and archives that provide high-impact dissemination and long-term preservation of scholarly information that benefits the academy and society.

The escalating costs of publications and increased publishers' restrictions on use have created a crisis in academic libraries' ability to acquire and provide access to research materials. To improve the situation, the UCI Libraries actively seek and support new publishing alternatives and business models that promote educational use and are economically sustainable.

I encourage you to consider two approaches: publishing in open-access journals with reasonable pricing models, and depositing articles in open archives in your discipline. The Libraries provide financial support by paying institutional memberships that provide significant discounts (ranging from 100% to 20%) to UC authors on publication fees for publications such as *Public Library of Science* journals, *Nucleic Acids Research,* the *Proceedings of the NationalAcademy of Science,* and *BioMed Central* journals. We also co-sponsor open-access journals such as those from Geometry & Topology Publications, Project Euclid, and many others. These publications' copyright agreements with authors generally enable broad dissemination and re-use of materials. Publication costs are supported by low subscription costs, author submission charges (usually covered by grant funds), and various types of subventions from scholars' home institution, libraries, or private funding. Open access is spreading to an expanding number of disciplines.

UC Discounts on Article Publication Charges
osc.universityofcalifornia.edu/alternatives/submit_work.html

Directory of Open Access Repositories
www.opendoar.org

Inside this issue

UCI Libraries Update

Contributors:
Anne Frank, Harold Gee
Carol Hughes, Susan Lessick
Gerald Munoff, Catherine
Palmer, Julie Sully, Mark Vega

Editor: Jackie Dooley

Design & Production:

National Institutes of Health Public Access Policy
www.lib.uci.edu/scamp/nihpolicy.html

Public Library of Science
www.plos.org

PubMed Central
www.pubmedcentral.nih.gov

Rigorous peer review and high standards are the hallmarks of a number of open-access publications. *Public Library of Science* is a prime example; others can be found in the Directory of Open Access Repositories. The National Institutes of Health recently issued its Public Access Policy that calls upon scientists who have received NIH funding to submit their publications to the PubMed Central open access archive within 12 months of final publication.

The UCI Libraries will assist academic units that wish to participate in the University of California's eScholarship repository, which provides open access to items such as pre-prints, post-prints, working papers, and seminar papers (see related article in the winter 2005 issue of *UCI Libraries Update*).

Open-access journals and archives increase information exchange among scholars, thus advancing research. They also make more resources available for instructional purposes and to the general public for the advancement of society. While open access may not solve the publishing crisis, with our support it has the potential to make a significant contribution.

SCAMP, the Libraries' Scholarly Communication and Management Program, provides contacts and more information.

Gerald J. Munoff
University Librarian

Volume 24, Number 3, Spring 2006

UCI Libraries Update

A Newsletter for Faculty

Volume 24, Number 3, Spring 2006

1 2 3 4 5 6 7 8 Next »

Message from the University Librarian: Partnerships to Digitize Print Collections

UC Irvine and the other University of California libraries have joined a partnership with Yahoo and other universities in the Open Content Alliance (OCA) to build an openly available digital library with materials drawn from across the world.

For UC's first project, all UC libraries will contribute books and resources to create a digital collection of out-of-copyright American literature. Other contributors will focus on different subjects and genres to expand the permanent archive of digitized multilingual text and multimedia content. Subsequent UC projects are planned to include American fiction, historical works of mathematics, and 19th Century British poetry.

This project differs significantly from the projects currently underway between a number of universities and Google. The OCA projects focus on discrete, coherent subject collections that are research focused, and, initially, out of copyright. The collections will offer full-text access, based on principles of non-exclusive use, and will be available to read, and in most cases, download or print, as determined by contributors. The OCA consortium is global and includes commercial partners in an open and collaborative process to create a world-class research and educational resource.

UCI Libraries' books will be digitized by the nonprofit Internet Archive using a new technology that scans books at a high rate of speed for lower costs than other

Inside this issue

UCI Libraries *Update*

Contributors:
Jackie Dooley, Julia Gelfand, Judd Nubert, Carol Hughes, Stephen MacLeod, Gerald Munoff, Cathy Palmer

Editor: Jackie Dooley

Design and Production:
Julia Crosara

Published three times annually by
The UC Irvine Libraries Design Services
(949) 824-6628

www.lib.uci.edu

processes. Books and other materials will not be dismantled or damaged in this process, as is sometimes the case in microfilming. The materials, indexed by Yahoo, will be available from the UCI Libraries website www.lib.uci.edu as well as at the Open Content Alliance website www.opencontentalliance.org.

OCA's other partners include Columbia University, the University of Texas, the University of Toronto, the National Library of Australia, the National Archives (U.K.), Microsoft, and Hewlett Packard. The OCA is continuing discussions with publishers to explore sustainable business models that allow more copyrighted content to be made widely available.

UCI Libraries are pleased to join the OCA and contribute to making our national intellectual and cultural heritage widely available online.

Gerald J. Munoff
University Librarian

http://library.duke.edu/blogs/scholcomm/category/open-access-and-institutional-repositories/

When should the government intervene?   September 13, 2007

Posted by Kevin Smith in : Copyright Issues and Legislation, Open Access and Institutional Repositories , add a comment

There has not been a lot of comment on this site about the launch of PRISM (The Partnership for Research Integrity in Science & Medicine – a coalition of publishing organizations that is campaigning against the proposals in Congress to require public access to federally-funded research. One reason for this lack of comment is that the actual arguments and assertions made by PRISM are so transparent and easily refuted; I called them simple-minded in an earlier post (here), and I have seen nothing that changes that judgment. Also, lots of other blogs and listservs have dealt extensively with the claims of PRISM, especially after the Director of Columbia University Press resigned from the Executive Council of the American Association of Publishers over its support of the Partnership and the Director of Cambridge University Press wrote a letter repudiating its absurd assertions (see news item in The Chronicle of Higher Education here).

But even a silly debate can produce significant points, and one of the most important contributions to this argument comes from William Patry, senior copyright counsel for Google, whose blog has been cited here several times before. The "PRISM principles" refer repeatedly to preventing "government intervention" in scientific research. The irony of complaining of government interference in research that is paid for from federal tax monies in the first place should be pretty obvious, but Patry adds another point that is worth our attention. As he says in this post, "Copyright is always Government Intervention." By definition, copyright is a government-granted monopoly that artificially supports the price of intellectual property to provide an incentive to creation. Patry nicely explains the logic behind this government intervention and the reasoning that underlies the attempt to create a balance between incentives for creators and opportunities for users.

However one feels about whether we have struck the appropriate balance in the US or have erred to one side or the other, most will agree that the economic rationale for copyright as a government intervention in the free market is sound. We can only wonder if PRISM however, will be true to its professed disdain for government measures and support the total abolition of copyright. Such a change would create a genuinely free market, where publishers would be free to compete with each other by publishing the same works at competitive prices; consumers would likely benefit from lower prices for books and movies, but it is pretty certain that creativity would suffer in the long run.

 Share This

What faculty think   September 11, 2007

Posted by Kevin Smith in : Open Access and Institutional Repositories, Scholarly Publishing, Technologies , 1 comment so far

It is always dangerous to try and speculate about the opinions and attitudes of a large group, especially one as diverse as university faculty. But the University of California's Office of Scholarly Communications always produces great research, and their recent report on "Faculty Attitudes and Behaviors Regarding Scholarly Communication" is no exception. The full report can be downloaded here, and a PDF of the Executive Summary and Summary of Findings is here. This is solid, empirical research that can help guide attempts to reform and renew the system of disseminating scholarly research.

One of the most interesting findings in this report is the disconnect it documents between attitudes and behaviors around open access and, especially, copyright. Faculty members

search [   ] [go!]

Categories
- Author Rights
- Commerce in the Classroom
- Copyright Issues and Legislation
- Digital Rights Management
- Fair Use
- Open Access and Institutional Repositories
- Scholarly Publishing
- Technologies

Recommended readings
- Open Access and the Arena of Electronic Publishing
- Influence in academia: tokens as scholarly publication & communication practices
- Will Fair Use Survive? – reprint from the Brennan Center for Justice
- "Big Deal" Bundling of Academic Journals
- Values and Journal Pricing model
- Report: Scholarly Communication: Academic Values and Sustainable Models
- University of California Whitepaper on Copyright Management
- Digital Learning Challenge
- SSRN Educational Fair Use in Copyright: Reclaiming the Right to Photocopy Essay by Ann Bartow
- Forecast for the by Michael Carroll

Recent Posts
- Student rights and academic values
- A first footnote
- When should the government intervene?
- What faculty think
- Copyright & the First Amendment
- Is this just scholarship?
- Stuck in the Copyright Wars
- Assessing and growing pains
- Where (and to) collaborate
- Can Google inform quality

Recent Comments
- Scholarly Communications @ Duke » A Sad Footnote on Stuck in the Copyright Wars
- Betsy Ferguson on What faculty think
- Kevin Smith on Jamming: out of proper points
- Kevin Smith » Copyright & the First Amendment on Copyright & the First Amendment
- Scholarly Communications @ Duke » When should the government intervene? on Values in the Copyright Wars

Archives
- September 2007
- August 2007
- July 2007
- June 2007
- May 2007
- April 2007
- March 2007
- February 2007
- January 2007
- December 2006

MASSACHUSETTS
INSTITUTE OF
TECHNOLOGY

MIT Faculty Newsletter

Vol. XVIII No. 4
March/April 2006

contents

A Failure in Communcations

The metamorphosis of academic publishing

Brian Evans

I really have to lean into the wind to make some headway as I come through the wind tunnel at the base of the building. Well, what do you expect? After all, it's March, and this is Building 54. Instead of waiting for the elevators, I decide to walk up to the seventh floor. There is not going to be any time for any other exercise today. How can you work for 12 hours each day, and get further and further behind?

Trudging up the stairs, I go over my list of things to do. Actually the hike is more like 10 floors, but my list is long enough to last the entire trip. On the way past the mail room, I grab my pile of incoming. Let's see: junk, junk, the *Faculty Newsletter* – put that aside to read cover to cover later – junk, junk, some papers to review, a few proposals to read, a couple of manuscripts to revise . . . Wait, what's this? A letter from the publisher. Great, our paper was accepted! Here's the copyright agreement. Man, who writes this stuff? Well, at least I can sign this, get it out of here, and get on with life. After all, you don't really have a choice about these agreements, right? There isn't anything you can do, and the media rights don't matter, anyway. Nobody's going to make a movie out of my research.

Well, actually, most of those comments are dead wrong. There is a choice, those agreements do matter, and you, the author, are not powerless. There are things you can do about it, but first, a little history.

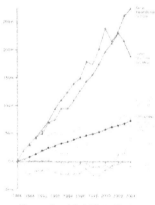

Monograph and Serial Expenditures
in ARL Libraries, 1986-2004
(click on image to enlarge)

For perhaps the last 10-15 years, academic publishing has been metamorphosing in dramatic fashion. Most of us are aware of the transition from print to electronic media. For those with the right institutional connections, access to most major research journals is now possible from our offices or, even, at home. Less apparent to end-users in academe has been the transfer of publication costs from the single subscriber to multiple-journal, multi-user access licenses by libraries, institutions, and systems. These fundamental changes in the business strategies of the commercial academic publishers have caused extraordinarily large increases of cost for colleges and universities (see graph). Additionally, globalization of the scholarly printing trade has dramatically reduced the number of publishers, even as the number of journals has increased.

Intellectual property rights are also in transition. The advent of the Internet and its promise of large amounts of freely accessible information have triggered a movement to replace copyright law with contract law. Access to scholarly publications is now rented yearly, rather than purchased.

The right to own print copies now incurs charges in addition to simple subscription costs, and many publishers are moving to eliminate traditional print versions entirely.

Thus, if a library drops a journal subscription, access to the entire electronic version may be lost, and recourse to a printed copy is much less likely. Subscription rates are now negotiated individually by institutions, rather than being based on standard values for all colleges. A small community college is likely to pay much less for a given journal than a major research institution. Of course, the research institution also has less flexibility in cutting important journals and, consequently, has less leverage in threatening to cut subscription costs. As publishers strive to protect access to journal content, the contract and copyright agreements have become much less standard and, generally, more restrictive.

[▲] Back to top

In response to these trends, a grass-root, "open-access" movement has developed with the loosely defined goal of providing freely accessible repositories of intellectual material, governed by less restrictive copyright assignments, as defined by a broader portion of the academic community (for example, see sciencecommons.org). The open-access movement is driven by a wide variety of forces, amongst which are desires for fewer restrictions on the use of published material in the classroom, increased accessibility, decreased cost, and greater clarity in copyright issues. Open access journals tend to be concentrated in, but not exclusively restricted to, health, medicine, and biological sciences. Concern for public access has been most visible in these medical fields, with the argument being made that access to publicly funded research should not be overly restricted by private copyright interests. Private funding foundations, including the Wellcome Trust, and other public agencies, e.g., the UK Research councils, are also moving in this direction. In the last year, the National Institutes of Health (NIH) have instituted a policy requesting deposit of final peer-reviewed manuscripts into a repository called PubMed Central (NLM). Although the NIH policy stops short of requiring deposits, submission is strongly encouraged.

But what, exactly, are the roles of MIT, its faculty, students, and researchers in all this? First, if the Institute can provide mechanisms to clarify copyright issues and to increase the efficiency of scholarly output of our staff and students, it should do so. Second, it is in the best interest of the Institute to retain control of its intellectual output while insuring broad dissemination, but only if it can be done in ways that are responsible to individual investigators, to the academic community, and to the general public. Finally, it is in the best interests of the entire academic community to encourage balance and cooperation amongst all members of the scholarly publishing community, whether private or public, and if MIT can provide leadership within academe, we should not shirk.

Fortunately, progress on the first item has been made. Owing to hard work on the part of Ann Wolpert and the staff of the MIT Library Systems, the Committee on Intellectual Property, Vice President for Research Alice Gast, and the Office of the Provost, there are now systems being developed to help investigators respond to the NIH policy. In part, the purpose of this article is simply to alert faculty and staff to the fact that there are some tools designed to help the individual investigator. One of the most recent developments is a standard amendment to publication agreements, drafted by the Intellectual Property Counsel, which is available online at *http://web.mit.edu/faculty/research.html*; *http://web.mit.edu/faculty/agreement.pdf*; *http://libraries.mit.edu/about/scholarly/amendment.doc*.

The last of these sites also has information about the open-access movement, clarification of the NIH initiative, and discussion of scholarly communications in general. The amendment to publication agreement provides a relatively easy method to standardize copyright assertions for your own work. In addition, library systems staff are available to assist NIH investigators and others in the submission of work to Dspace. Bearing in mind that Dspace is available for all MIT faculty members, such a repository could be used for a much broader spectrum of the research output of the MIT community, an option that is particularly attractive given the commitment of Dspace to providing a robust and durable Website with upward migration of data.

Progress in the broader community is also possible, I believe. With increased awareness of the issues confronting academic publishing, MIT faculty are in a position to exert responsible leadership with our colleagues at other universities. Tempting as it might be to grab pitchforks and torches and march off to man the barricades, we, as a faculty, need to be thoughtful and constructive in our approach. What we cannot do with any sense of collective responsibility is simply watch. The issues are too important for scientific and engineering research, for universities and colleges, and for the fulfillment of MIT's core mission, to allow outside forces to decide the outcome. It is time for a broad discussion involving a large portion of the faculty and staff to formulate a constructive statement of policy. With general faculty support and awareness, we can exert force for positive change.

Sadly, though, I have been forced to realize it is probably true that no one is going to make a movie of my research. What a shame! Harrison Ford would have been perfect for the lead.

Back to top

Send your comments

home   this issue   archives   editorial board   contact us   faculty website

MIT Libraries News

MIT Student Day of Action for Open Access

Posted February 21st, 2007 by Ellen Duranceau

MIT students supported a national effort when they carried out a â€œday of action for open accessâ€ on the MIT campus February 15.

Inspired by the National Day of Action for Open Access (sponsored by freeculture.org and the Alliance for Taxpayer Access), a group of students devised a project called â€œOverprice Tags.â€

The students who worked on the project were Benjamin Mako Hill (who goes by Mako) and Annina Rust (both pictured below) along with Noah Vawter, all graduate students in the Media Lab's Computing Culture group, as well as Daniel Jared Dominguez and Christine Sprang, both undergraduates. They created unique price tags and affixed them to the 100 journals they identified as costing MIT more that $5,000 per year.

Their goal, according to Hill, was to â€œbring attention to the open access issue and the sky-rocketing price of scholarly journals at MIT,â€ as well as to focus attention on â€œcompelling, publicly accessible alternatives to â€¦ closed and restrictive models of academic publishing.â€

Focusing on journal prices was a way to â€œgrab the attention of people who were unawareâ€ of the barriers to accessing research. As Hill notes, price is one of the barriers, but not the only one. Once they caught a readerâ€™s attention by â€œlooking a magazine with a $25,000 price tag,â€ Hillâ€™s group hoped that readers would be interested enough to follow the link to the "overprice tags" website, where they could â€œstart a real explanation of what the issues are.â€

Thought to be the â€œfirst major MIT Free Culture event,â€ this student day of action has already raised awareness on campus. All responses received so far have been supportive of the project, and many writers expressed interest in getting more involved in events related to open access.

For those who would like more information about open access or ideas about how to get involved, Hillâ€™s Open Access at MIT, and the Librariesâ€™ scholarly publishing web site offer summaries of the issues, links to groups who are involved, and recommended actions. You may also be interested in viewing a short slideshow of the MIT Student Day of Action for Open Access.

News Home
MIT Libraries News is powered by WordPress.
RSS Subscribe to our RSS feed.

http://library.syr.edu/information/libassoc/connection/winter0304.pdf

THE library
CONNECTION

News from the Syracuse University Library

FROM THE UNIVERSITY LIBRARIAN

The Public Library of Science (PLoS) is an example of a new open-access initiative. "PLoS is a nonprofit scientific publishing venture that provides scientists with high-quality, high-profile journals in which to publish their work, while making the full contents freely available online, with no charges for access and no restrictions on subsequent redistribution or use." *(from the PLoS web site; image courtesy of PLoS.)*

Open Access to Scholarship— New Opportunities for the University

New ideas are fermenting in the scholarly communication world. Terms such as open access, institutional and disciplinary repositories, and self-archiving are common currency today, not only on campuses but also in major scholarly journals, such as Nature, and at scholarly organizations, such as the American Council of Learned Societies. Scholars, researchers, and faculty are bubbling with ideas for using networked technologies to increase the speed and ease of communicating research results while decreasing costs. Syracuse University can play a leadership role in these new developments. In this issue, we propose two ways to do so.

The idea of open access is at the heart of the new ferment. Open access, in the academic networked world, refers to scholarly work made available for education and research at no cost to the reader, with a presumption that the work was created with no expectation of direct monetary return (as is the case with most scholarly work).

OBSTACLES TO ACCESS

Such an arrangement contrasts to the predominant publishing mode, which requires libraries to buy expensive subscriptions to journals, and thus to pay for access to what scholars have contributed to those journals for free.

Most scholars are now familiar with the crisis in journals: libraries are spending three times as much as 15 years ago for fewer journals (see chart, p. 2) and, consequently, are buying many fewer books. Mergers and acquisitions among publishers have reduced the 13 major STM (Science, Technology, Medicine) publishers of five years ago to only seven now, and their announced annual profit rates are in

the 20 to 35 percent range. Increasingly, libraries are only able to license—rather than purchase—journal content, which further restricts scholarly use. Large publishers are also pushing libraries into bundling agreements so that, as library budgets tighten, they are forced to cancel individual journals from smaller publishers.

New copyright legislation has put constraints on fair use. Publishers have worked with the entertainment industry to limit the "right of first sale," which lets the purchaser of a book lend it or give it away. This right is no longer available at all for digital information. Database legislation is being introduced to make facts protected by law!

OPEN-ACCESS PUBLICATION

Open access is a mode of publishing in which authors retain control over the copyright of their work, while making it freely available to the widest possible readership. Authors can transfer to publishers the rights to post on the web or to publish first in a journal, and can also retain the right to post work themselves, use it as they see fit, and retain control over its integrity. (If an author seeks financial gain from a work, she or he remains free to negotiate those rights with a publisher, as now.)

The intent is to provide information free to readers; however, there are some costs. Models have been proposed that put the costs at the front end, rather like page charges. The Wellcome Institute and the Howard Hughes Medical Institute have already committed to paying the up-front charges for their staff's contributions to open-access journals and to disciplinary repositories. These charges cover necessary administrative and technology costs.

OUR VISION

Our vision of Syracuse University Library—its people, services, collections, and facilities—is of a nationally significant research library that understands the needs of its users and has actively developed the resources and methods to meet those needs now and in the future.

Goal 7.1: Information Technology Implementation for Optimum User Access

Ensure proactive application of the information technologies required to create, integrate, organize, and customize online services and information resources in all formats.

Targets for Transformation, the Library's strategic plan (revised July 2002)

Currently, there are more than 500 open-access journals. A recent, well-publicized example is PLoS Biology, published by the Public Library of Science. Others include some supported by the Scholarly Publishing and Academic Resources Coalition (SPARC, of which the Library is a paying member), such as Documenta Mathematica and New Journal of Physics.

INSTITUTIONAL REPOSITORIES

Other open-access implementations include institutional and disciplinary repositories. The best known of the latter is the arXiv.org e-Print service, for preprints in high-energy physics and related disciplines, formerly at Los Alamos, and now hosted by Cornell University. BioMed Central publishes more than 50 online journals in biology and medicine, and provides open access on the web.

M.I.T. and the University of Southampton have each created open-source institutional repository software, now in use at dozens of universities around the U.S., from CalTech to Hofstra, and around the world (see the Open Archives Initiative URL for links to many of them). M.I.T.'s DSpace hosts research and teaching material from its own faculty, allowing researchers to select access levels to items they contribute (Southampton's EPrints is similar, but more discipline-based).

An institutional repository highlights the serious academic accomplishments of the institution: research and teaching tools are collocated in one place for all to see. Of equal importance, an institutional archive contributes to a new global system of distributed, interoperable repositories, helping to change the model of scholarly communication.

The growth of repositories has been accompanied by the development of harvesting tools—tools that let a scholar search over the aggregate of institutional archives using one command, rather like Google, but with better results. The convergence of possibilities

means that the present costly and constraining publishing model can be changed for the benefit of all scholars and students, and with a net reduction in cost of dissemination.

WHAT CAN WE DO HERE?

What role does Syracuse University want to play in shaping the future of research dissemination?

First of all, we need to talk about the new publishing models. Reasonable questions arise concerning peer review, effects on promotion and tenure, the relative status of major disciplinary journals and the new open-access journals, faculty retention of intellectual property rights, costs (to whom?), and disturbing the existing publishing model, which has taken centuries to build.

What about long-term digital preservation? What does it mean to make institutions, instead of publishers and scholarly societies, responsible for scholarly output? Are multiple solutions possible? Faculty must feel comfortable with new modes if they are to have any chance of success.

We in the Library have particular skills and knowledge to bring to these discussions. SU's Computing and Media Services will contribute its skills and knowledge to building the infrastructure. SU Press, the University Art Collection, and University Archives can bring important resources to the digital table. The college deans and the University administration should be involved from the beginning, which we believe should be soon.

It may now be time for SU faculty to join in supporting the open-access journal movement. To that end, the Library proposes for the next three years to subsidize the publication charges for articles by SU faculty published in open-access journals and disciplinary repositories. There is much to be worked out, and we look forward to discussions among faculty and the departments most affected on such questions as these: What defines an open-access journal? Should subventions be faculty-based or article-based? What limits can or should there be? What should the budget model eventually be? The Library will initiate forums and discussions during the spring 2004 semester. Interested faculty may contact Peter McDonald, associate University librarian for collection development, at x2977 or apmcdona@ syr.edu.

—Peter S. Graham
University Librarian

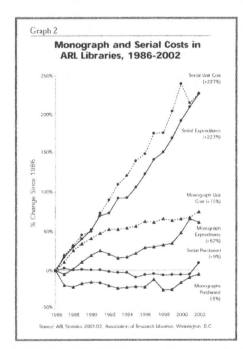

Graph 2

Monograph and Serial Costs in ARL Libraries, 1986-2002

Serial Unit Cost (+227%)
Serial Expenditures (+227%)
Monograph Unit Cost (+75%)
Monograph Expenditures (+62%)
Serial Purchased (+9%)
Monographs Purchased (-5%)

% Change Since 1986

Source: ARL Statistics 2001-02. Association of Research Libraries, Washington, D.C.

http://library.syr.edu/information/libassoc/connection/winter0304.pdf

New Initiatives in Open Access

Visit these web sites to learn more about open access:

Budapest Open-Access Initiative (BOAI) is a statement of principle, strategy, and commitment to making research articles in all academic fields publicly available on the Internet. The initiative has been endorsed by a growing number of researchers, universities, laboratories, libraries, foundations, journals, publishers, learned societies, and scholars from around the world. The BOAI recommends using two complementary strategies: self-archiving in institutional/disciplinary repositories and open-access journals. http://www.soros.org/openaccess/

SPARC (Scholarly Publishing and Academic Resources Coalition) is actively promoting both open-access journals and the development of institutional repositories. Developed by the research library community—including SU Library—SPARC has a number of open-access partners, including Algebraic and Geometric Topology, Documenta Mathematica, eScholarship, Geometry & Topology, and Journal of Insect Science. http://www.arl.org/sparc

Public Library of Science (PLoS) began as a grassroots initiative, signed by more than 30,000 scientists, to encourage publishers to deposit their journals in central archives, such as PubMed Central, within six months of publication. Having generated only modest response from publishers, the leaders of the PLoS are developing their own set of open-access journals (PLoS Biology has just appeared). http://www.publiclibraryofscience.org/

Berlin Declaration on Open Access to Knowledge in the Sciences and Humanities is an October 2003 statement of many European research organizations (e.g., CNRS, Max Planck Society). It supports open access, encourages scholars to so publish, and encourages experiments in funding and support. http://www.zim.mpg.de/openaccess-berlin/berlindeclaration.html

Open Archives Initiative (OAI, supported by NSF and the Digital Library Federation) develops and promotes interoperability standards that aim to facilitate the efficient dissemination of content. The OAI has its roots in an effort to enhance access to e-print archives as a means of increasing the availability of scholarly communication. The fundamental technological framework and standards that are developing to support this work are, however, independent of both the type of content offered and the economic mechanisms surrounding that content. They promise to have much broader relevance in opening up access to a range of digital materials. OAI is committed to exploring and enabling this new and broader range of applications. http://www.openarchives.org

Oxford University Press has partnered with Oxford's Library to provide an institutional e-print archive with online access to articles by Oxford University-based authors, free of charge to researchers across the globe. http://www.sherpa.ac.uk/

Bibliography on Open Access

Here are citations and links to much more information about open access, repositories, and new modes of scholarly communication.

The Open Archives Initiative link above will lead to a list of more than 400 existing repositories. Some of the better known among them are the following:

Dspace at M.I.T. (https://dspace.mit.edu/index.jsp)

Collection of Digital Archives (CODA) at CalTech (http://library.caltech.edu/digital/)

Eprints.org, at the University of Southampton, is home source for over 100 repositories.

A directory of more than 500 open-access journals may be found at http://www.doaj.org/.

A registry of institutional repositories and open archives may be found at http://gita.grainger.uiuc.edu/registry/.

Extensive further information and bibliography on open access issues may be found on the Library Open Access web page at libwww.syr.edu/publications/openaccess.

Institutional Support for OA Authors

UNIVERSITY OF CALIFORNIA

http://osc.universityofcalifornia.edu/alternatives/submit_work.html

Reshaping Scholarly Communication

▸ Publisher and Journal Profiles ▸ Model Copyright Clauses

UNIVERSITY of CALIFORNIA
Office of Scholarly Communication

Home > Use Alternative Forms of Publishing > Submit to Open Access Journals   Search | Site Map

Submit to Open Access Journals

Open access journals are peer-reviewed journals that provide free, online access to their articles. They do not charge subscription fees to readers or libraries, rather, they cover costs through publication fees, institutional subsidies, endowments, or sponsorships. There are more than 1200 open access peer-reviewed scholarly journals. There are also hybrid models that allow open access to some of their material and recover their costs from a mixture of author charges, institutional memberships and print subscriptions.

See the list of UC discounts on publication fees below, a description of this and other alternatives and our table of the characteristics of scholarly publishing options.

Submission to an open access journal is certain to remove the financial access barriers for potential readers of your work. Although open access journals are relatively new, evidence to date suggests that publishing with them may increase the reach and impact of your work.

To help you consider submitting your work to these journals:

- Take advantage of the following UC institutional memberships:

UC Discounts on Article Publication Charges for Open Access Journals - 2007 (revised 8/21/07)

Publisher or Publication	Normal publication fee	UC discounted fee	Based on
BioMed Central (all BioMed Central journals)	~ $1375 average "Article Processing Fee"	~ $1170 (15% discount)	Supporting membership; Reveiwers for articles receive 20% discount for their own articles
Nucleic Acids Research (from Oxford Univ. Press)	$1900	$950 (50% discount)	Institutional memberships
Proceedings of the National Academy of Science (PNAS)	$1000 (to provide open access; separate from page and other charges)	$750 (25% discount)	Included as part of UC's online subscription
Public Library of Science	$1250 - $2750	10% discount	UC-affiliated corresponding author; Institutional membership

- Consult the list of more than 2,800 peer-reviewed open access journals, many with citation rates and impact factors equivalent or better than their traditional subscription-based counterparts, that are focused on increasing dissemination and experimenting with new business models. More appear every month. See the directory of open access journals.

RESEARCH AT CAROLINA

UNC-Chapel Hill Open Access Authors' Fund

About the Fund

- Provides support for publishing charges related to offering free immediate open access to journal articles
- Eligible authors are UNC-CH faculty, post-doctoral researchers, and graduate or professional students without grant funds to cover publication fees
- Award maximum is $1000 per article
- Sponsored by the Office of the Vice Chancellor for Research and Economic Development
- Managed by the Health Sciences Library and the Academic Affairs Library

Retrieve a copy of the application.

Open access authors' fees at core journal publishers

- American Chemical Society *Author Choice*
  Open access is $1,000 for ACS members affiliated with an ACS subscribing institution.
- Proceedings of the National Academy of Science
  Open access surcharge of $750 provides immediate open access for authors at any institution with a site license. All articles are free online after 6 months.
- Public Library of Science
  PLoS Biology and PLoS Medicine are $2500; PLoS Computational Biology, PLoS Genetics and PLoS Pathogens are $2000; institutional membership reduces a UNC-CH corresponding author's fee by 15%.
- Use the Directory of Open Access Journals to find more.

Why choose open access?

"Providing OA to your own work is not an act of charity that only benefits others, or a sacrifice justified only by the greater good. It's not a sacrifice at all. It increases your visibility, retrievability, audience, usage, and citations. It's about career-building. For publishing scholars, it would be a bargain even if it were costly, difficult, and time-consuming." Suber

More information about open access publishing

See the Health Sciences Library Open Access and Scholarly Communications website.

Vice Chancellor Tony Waldrop established The Open Access Fund in March 2005 at the request of University Librarian Sarah Michalak and Health Sciences Library Director Carol Jenkins. The University Libraries are committed to raising awareness among the faculty about open access and open archive publishing alternatives and helping to pay the associated publication costs.

WAYNE STATE UNIVERSITY

http://www.lib.wayne.edu/geninfo/about/scholarly_communications/publishing.php

Open Access Publishing at WSU

Wayne State University Library System Supports Open Access

To encourage our faculty and students to consider Open Access publication, increase access to their publications and to heighten awareness of the crisis in scholarly and scientific communication, the University Libraries have expanded their support with new local and national initiatives:

Memberships Eliminate or Decrease Manuscript Charges for WSU Authors

Biomed Central - An independent publisher of open access journals, with rapid peer review and without the need for copyright transfer, WSU authors can publish accepted manuscripts at no charge. Wayne State University's membership eliminates charges that can range from $580.00 to $1665.00 per article. Annual subscriptions to databases including ImagesMD, Faculty of 1000, a version of PubMed with post-publication commentaries by world-wide faculty and these journals also represent the libraries commitment to supporting our faculty and students.

Nucleic Acids Research - Beginning in 2005, *Nucleic Acids Research* became a fully open access journal. The University Libraries membership on behalf of WSU authors reduces the 2006 accepted manuscript charge to $950.00 from $1900.00.

Proceedings of the National Academy of Sciences of the USA - The Libraries' annual site license to *PNAS* provides WSU authors with a 25% reduction in the cost of making articles freely available. Please see publication charges.

Important National Initiatives

The **National Institutes of Health's** Policy on Enhancing Public Access to Archived Publications Resulting from NIH-Funded Research seeks to enhance the public's access to publications derived from NIH-supported research. NIH requests and strongly encourages all investigators to make their nih-funded peer-reviewed, author's final manuscript available through the National Library of Medicine's free digital archive PubMed Central immediately after the final date of journal publication. Manuscript submission is easy, taking only a few minutes. For assistance with submission, contact the Shiffman Medical Library staff at askmed@wayne.edu

WSU authors are also encouraged to examine the publishing potential in the **Public Library of Science (PLOS)**. These journals currently include *PLOS Biology*, *PLOS Medicine*, *PLOS Computational Biology*, *PLOS Genetics*, and *PLOS Pathogens* and *PLOS Clinical Trials*, which seeks to overcome publication bias in clinical trials.

Wayne State University is a charter supporter of **BioOne**, a non-profit publishing venture for the benefit of scientific societies, universities, libraries, scholars and students. Our support provides the WSU community with access to BioOne's biological and environmental sciences journals.

Wayne State University Supports Open Access Organizations

WSU is a member of the **Coalition for Networked Information** (CNI), a scholarly organization dedicated to supporting the transformative promise of networked information technology for the advancement of scholarly communication and the enrichment of intellectual productivity. In addition to conferences and current awareness listservs, CNI publishes significant white papers and monographs -- available online.

The **Scholarly Publishing and Academic Resources Coalition** (SPARC) and **SPARC Europe** are alliances of academic and research libraries and organizations working to correct the market dysfunction in the scholarly publication system. Wayne State University is a full member of this organization that provides resources for advocacy, education, and alternative models of publication.

Local Initiatives

The Wayne State University Library System has embarked on the development of an institutional repository, (Digital Commons@Wayne) a digital archive designed for open access to university scholarship and research. Currently in its development phases, interested faculty and staff are encouraged to contact Nardina Mein .

University Libraries' catalogers have made a strategic effort to promote access to open access journals in all disciplines. Open access journals are accessible through the Libraries' catalog and through the alphabetic list of online journals.

For More Information

For an overview of the crisis in scholarly communication and what faculty and campuses can do, please see *Create Change* and for concrete action steps see *Open Access*.

Contacts

Nardina Mein, LCMS Director

Ellen Marks, Medical Library Director

OA Collection Development Policies

 **LIBRARIES**   Search   Databases   Journals   Services   Ask Us

Home | My Account | FAQ | About Us | Version française | University of Alberta

You are here: Home » About Us » Our Collection »
Collection Policy

University of Alberta Libraries Collection Development Policy

November, 2006

This policy establishes the overall selection standards and criteria for the acquisition of library materials. The collection policies of the individual area libraries describe the scope of the collections under their administration.

The University of Alberta Libraries exist primarily to support the University's teaching and research functions and to provide an information source for University staff and the general public. As the repository of one of the major Canadian research collections, the Library also serves the needs of the wider regional, national and international communities. This policy acknowledges the need to rely on cooperative resource-sharing activities to extend the breadth and depth of our collections.

Collection management at the University of Alberta is the responsibility of professional library staff. This function is carried out in consultation with faculty, students and other users. To contact the librarian responsible for collecting materials in your subject area, please visit Liaison Librarians.

The University of Alberta Library subscribes to the professional codes and standards adopted by the Canadian Library Association including the Statement of Intellectual Freedom.

We are committed to the principles of open access, as outlined in the *IFLA Statement on Open Access to Scholarly Literature and Research Documentation*. Open access (OA) benefits researchers and learners by equalizing access to research information and facilitating scholarly communication. The University of Alberta Libraries include OA products in our collections, and provide support for members of the University of Alberta community who want to publish in OA formats. For more information about open access, please contact your liaison librarian.

General Criteria for Selection of Library Materials

The library will consider acquiring information in any format needed to support the University's academic programs. The following criteria are considered by librarians in the selection of material:

1. Support of both current and future research or teaching needs.
2. Appropriateness for graduate or undergraduate programs, and/or research at the University of Alberta.
3. Quality of the material.
4. Minimal duplication of materials among the libraries.
5. Accessibility of appropriate material at other institutions.
6. Type and cost of support needed for materials selected.
7. Gift and free materials will be considered for inclusion in the collection according to the same selection criteria used for decisions to purchase materials. (Information about Donations)

Collections Policies

- Augustana Faculty Library
- Bibliotheque St. Jean
- Canadian Circumpolar Collection
- Herbert T. Coutts Library
- Humanities and Social Sciences Library
- John A. Weir Memorial Library
- John W. Scott Health Sciences Library
- Science and Technology Library
- William C. Wonders Map Collection

http://libraries.universityofcalifornia.edu/cdc/principlesforacquiring.html

The UNIVERSITY *of* CALIFORNIA LIBRARIES

Home | Search

UC Libraries Home > About the UC Libraries > Systemwide Groups and Activities > Systemwide Operations and Planning Advisory Group (SOPAG) > Collection Development Committee (CDC)

- About the UC Libraries
- Universitywide Planning & Action
- Libraries & Scholarly Communication
- Campus Libraries

Principles for Acquiring and Licensing Information in Digital Formats

University of California Libraries
Collection Development Committee
July, 2006

Preamble

The University of California continually expands and evolves its strategic approach to building well organized, professionally managed, comprehensive collections of information needed to realize the goals of the University's academic programs and its public service mission. The University of California Libraries collections strategy is to carefully coordinate and collaboratively manage a variety of library collections, including both those held in common and those held by a single campus that are shared across the university.

Comprehensive collections that meet the University's mission cannot be continuously assembled when scholarly publications are offered only at hyper-inflating subscription prices. Therefore, the University and its libraries also have a strategic interest in advancing a marketplace for scholarly materials that is economically balanced and sustainable.

The following principles are provided to inform and guide the University and its employees (at both campus and university-wide levels) in their business relationships with providers of scholarly information in digital formats.

These principles replace the University of California Libraries Principles For Acquiring And Licensing Information In Digital Formats 1996. The UC libraries have benefited from, and seek to contribute to the academic library community's longstanding efforts in the identification and promulgation of collection development principles for digital materials.

Further information about how the UC libraries operationalize these principles is contained in the California Digital Library's Checklist of Points to be Addressed in a CDL License Agreement and in the full text of the CDL Standard License Agreement available on the CDL website.

1) COLLECTION DEVELOPMENT

   a. Collection development criteria pertaining to quality and relevance should be paramount and should be applied consistently across formats, including digital resources.

   b. Digital materials should be at least equivalent to their print counterparts, if such exist, i.e. they should be complete and able to be considered and managed as a copy of record.

   c. Balance must be maintained among:
- disciplines;
- instructional and research tools;
- the differing needs of each campus.

   d. UC should retain authority for selecting and deselecting materials. Its selection prerogative covers content decisions at the title level and preferences of format and should not be compromised by provider-defined connections between titles or between print and digital products.

   e. UC will evaluate the cost/benefits of licensing digital resources of out of copyright information against opportunities to digitize equivalent UC resources or participate in other non-profit third-party digitizing efforts of that information.

UNIVERSITY OF CALIFORNIA

2) COSTS & PRICING

a. UC seeks and encourages methods for pricing electronic content that balance the financial requirements of information providers and the budgets and mission of the UC libraries. UC will give preference to vendors and products that have, or are developing, business models and practices that are economically sustainable for UC. Sustainable practices include reasonable absolute price changes, and explicit and reasonable bases for price changes, ideally reflecting actual amortized and/or operating costs.

b. The price of a resource to UC should be aligned with its value to UC. Value is necessarily multi-variate, including but not limited to use, price-per-page, price-per-citation, impact factor, and relevance to UC academic programs. UC will endeavor to refine indicators of value and to share the use of those indicators with resource providers.

c. Publishers can and should gain operational efficiencies, particularly in the marginal costs of adding and distributing content. These efficiency gains should be passed on to customers in the form of significant reductions in the "unit-cost" of information. Publishers should be discouraged from increasing prices to amortize print to digital conversion costs over short timeframes.

d. Content and access costs should be separated. UC should have flexibility in selecting appropriate access mechanisms and levels and should be able to alter these agreements for an existing license, subject only to access and use restrictions in the license agreement. Where possible, business terms should separate content pricing from pricing for access.

e. Because UC has a coordinated and collaboratively managed variety of library collections and services in which the collections of the individual campuses are enriched by capabilities to access the resources of all the others, "cross-access" should be a contractual option. Cross-access business terms should be based on actual or realistic estimates of UC audience, account for the fact that the university is a single system, and acknowledge efficiencies in conducting business with one rather than multiple (campus) parties.

3) TRANSFORMATIVE STRATEGIES

a. The libraries make principled investments in publishing business models that produce high quality scholarly content and have the potential for transforming scholarly communication. A publishing or distribution effort can be considered transformative when it is developed principally to reduce access barriers (e.g. open access models), to provide an alternative to expensive for-profit efforts, and to establish long-term economic sustainability (e.g. by redistributing production costs) that is affordable by libraries.

b. UC consideration of scholarly publishing endeavors is informed by endorsements and analyses by key organizations supporting transformative models such as the Scholarly Publishing and Academic Resources Coalition (SPARC) and the International Coalition of Library Consortia (ICOLC).

c. UC encourages publishers who develop scholarly communication models that represent innovative forms of quality or peer review processes and new publication modalities. Products should leverage technology for efficiencies in production, timely distribution, and integration with other resources.

d. UC-affiliated authors are major contributors to scholarly journals and other publications whose content is licensed by the UC libraries for teaching, research and patient care purposes. The libraries support the right of UC authors whose scholarly work is included in materials licensed by UC to retain copyright to their work, transferring only first-publication and/or commercial use rights to the publisher while retaining all other non-commercial use and distribution rights.

4) LICENSING

a. Information providers should employ a standard agreement that contains all of the elements of UC's Model License Agreement, which describes the rights of libraries and their authorized users in terms that are readable and explicit. Permitted uses should include standard academic practices such as interlibrary loan, the inclusion of materials in printed and online coursepacks and reserve reading lists, and ad-hoc sharing of individual items by scholars and researchers.

b. As a public institution with a broad mandate to serve the State of California, UC's "authorized users" include faculty, staff, students and all on-site users of the UC facility. UC's "site" includes every location, physically and virtually, maintained by UC for use by a bona fide member of the UC community. UC makes a good faith effort to authenticate authorized users. UC takes privacy concerns seriously and will not implement systems that abridge or threaten personal privacy. UC will work with and give preference to vendors that have, or are dedicated to developing scalable models for authentication.

c. UC requires business terms that provide for perpetual access by the approved community of users to content that has been purchased or licensed at any point in time. Contracts should specify the means and responsibilities for providing perpetual access in the event that a resource is subsequently canceled or removed by the vendor.

d. Licenses should provide for archival deposit of perpetually-licensed content in one or more third-party trusted digital preservation repositories to safeguard the long-term integrity of the material. The preservation repository should comply with the emerging standards for digital preservation such as the Open Archival Information System (OAIS) Reference Model and the RLG/NARA Audit Checklist for the Certification of Trusted Digital Repositories.

e. Vendors should also provide a means for UC to take possession of the complete digital files of perpetually-licensed content, at the university's option, either for business reasons or as a means to provide perpetual access. Business terms define appropriate uses of such archival copies.

f. UC affirms the importance of fair use in fulfilling its libraries' missions and requires that licenses not abrogate the rights allowed it or its members under copyright law, including, but not limited to, fair use and inter-library loan.

5) FUNCTIONALITY & INTEROPERABILITY

a. UC use data compliant with COUNTER standards should be available to UC as part of contractual provisions for a license. The confidentiality of individual users and their searches must be fully protected. Use data generated by UC may be available to the information provider.

b. UC will give preference to products whose design and architecture do not constrain access and service integration. Characteristics of such products include explicit and industry standard data formats, support for metadata and data export, and methods for interoperability such as application program interfaces (APIs) and reference (OpenURL) linking.

c. Interfaces should conform to industry standards (including performance standards), concentrate on known functional requirements, and avoid the unnecessary proliferation of platforms. UC should share usability findings and functional requirements information with vendors.

d. Information providers must keep UC informed of format and content changes and coordinate their implementation with UC.

More detailed information about UC functionality requirements can be found at http://cdlib.org/vendors/.

Comments and suggestions are welcome and should be addressed to the Collection Development Committee (see http://libraries.universityofcalifornia.edu/cdc/).

A PDF version of this document is available.

RELEVANT LINKS:

UC-Focused

Checklist of Points to be Addressed in a CDL License Agreement.
http://www.cdlib.org/vendors/checklist.html

[The Regents Of The University Of California.] Standard License Agreement.
http://www.cdlib.org/vendors/CDLModelLicense.rtf

Joint Steering Committee for Shared Collections. Factors to Consider When Licensing Out-of-Copyright Materials
http://cdlib.org/inside/collect/outofcopyright.rtf

http://libraries.universityofcalifornia.edu/cdc/principlesforacquiring.html

Other

Counting Online Usage of Networked Electronic Resources (COUNTER).
http://www.projectcounter.org/

International Coalition of Library Consortia (ICOLC).
http://www.library.yale.edu/consortia/

RLG/NARA Audit Checklist for the Certification of Trusted Digital
Repositories.
http://www.rlg.org/en/page.php?Page_ID=20769

SPARC (Scholarly Publishing and Academic Resources Coalition).
http://www.arl.org/sparc/

Document owner: Martha Ramirez
Last reviewed: September, 25, 2007

Comments? Feedback?

Factors to Consider When Licensing Out-of-Copyright Materials

California Digital Library
Joint Steering Committee for Shared Collections - July 2006

A number of recent announcements of mass digitization projects that include out-of-copyright material are challenging our collective decision-making process when these same materials are available in a commercially licensed product. The SLASIAC 2005 progress report on *Systemwide Strategic Directions For Libraries And Scholarly Information* called attention to this issue, referring to the UC's participation in large-scale digitization efforts as potentially offering opportunities for "reducing expenditures on vendor products that are based on out-of-copyright and other public domain materials." Do we license a commercial version of out-of-copyright content when a digitized version is already openly available? How do we assess whether an open digitized version is sufficiently robust to meet UC's needs? Do we license content to satisfy the immediate needs of UC faculty and students when future digitization projects promise open access? With such prospects in view, should we choose a time-limited subscription to the licensed version over perpetual ownership rights in order to contain our costs? When do we choose to digitize out-of-copyright materials ourselves or with partners using existing UC collections in preference to licensing? Conversely, when is it more cost-effective to license material instead of building it? The SLASIAC report challenges us to incorporate such considerations in our decision process for licensing materials in the public domain.

Evaluation Criteria

Standard evaluation criteria should be applied to any resource under consideration, whether licensed or open access. These include the UC *Principles for Acquiring and Licensing Materials in Digital Formats* and the more specific criteria outlined in documents such as the CDL Technical Requirements for Vendors, CDL Resource Selection Criteria, and the CDL Licensing Checklist. Given the intrinsic benefits of lower cost and barrier-free access that open content initiatives promise, such evaluations necessarily take on a new dimension when competing licensed and open access versions are available. For example, if material is held in an analog format and is (or is planned to be) also available in an open access form, licensing yet another version may warrant special scrutiny or justification.

In the course of evaluating any new resource for systemwide licensing, many individuals and groups will usually be involved:

- bibliographer groups who submit the original request
- CDL staff analyzing campus requests
- JSC in prioritizing requests
- JSC in prioritizing requests

When evaluating requests for systemwide licensing of new resources that include out-of-copyright material, the following factors should be considered by each group involved at the various stages of evaluation:

- Whether an alternative open access version exists or is planned
- Whether UC is actively pursuing or considering a digitization opportunity for the same material, either alone or collaboratively (e.g. CDL-built content through OCA)
- If a future open access version is anticipated, the value of access to content now vs. open access at some point in the future. Factors to consider might include, for example, the level or urgency of user demand and/or potential near-term cost savings through print deduplication and/or remote storage
- A careful appraisal of whether there is sufficient added value in the licensed version to justify the expenditure of scarce collection dollars when an alternative version exists. Factors to critically evaluate in this light might include:
  - The value derived from a relationship to other currently-licensed material (e.g. backfiles of currently-licensed journals where access may be integrated
  - Aggregation of content under a single interface as opposed to independently-created digitized versions that lack coordinated access
  - Indexing and presentation of content, or other added features that enhance the end user experience. Recognizing end users' increasing preference for 'single search box' simplicity in accessing content, careful judgments should be made about whether an open access resource

is adequate to satisfy the bulk of UC student and faculty needs

- The degree to which the licensed resource adheres to UC licensing and technical requirements. Nonconformity that might be overlooked when alternatives are unavailable may be less acceptable in the face of open access.

Next Steps

While we recognize that it is 'early days' in the emerging relationship between licensed and open content, the UC libraries' stated interest in developing a more holistic approach to collection development across these domains requires us to increasingly engage such questions. As a first step, bibliographers should attempt to identify relevant open access projects and opportunities in their areas of expertise and address the above criteria in any licensing recommendations submitted to JSC. The CDL licensed content and built content programs will also begin consulting regularly to identify synergies with digitizing initiatives. As we begin to incorporate these criteria in decisions that include public domain content, our collective understanding of these issues and their interplay will increase.

References:

Systemwide Strategic Directions For Libraries And Scholarly Information. Progress Report [2005]. **http://libraries.universityofcalifornia.edu/planning/SSD_progress_report_2005_final.pdf**

Principles for Acquiring and Licensing Materials in Digital Formats. **http://libraries.universityofcalifornia.edu/cdc/principles.html**

CDL Technical Requirements for Vendors. **http://cdlib.org/vendors/#technical**

CDL Licensing Checklist. **http://cdlib.org/vendors/checklist.html**

Document owner: **Wendy Parfrey**
Last reviewed: August 7, 2006
URL: http://www.cdlib.org/inside/collect/outofcopyright.html

Contact the CDL

- *Collection development and licensing staff:* [**HTML**]
- *Campus Acquisitions Liaisons:* [**HTML**]
- *UC Bibliographer Group Chairs and JSC Liasons:* [**RTF**]
- *Obtain access to* [password-protected] *areas of the web site:* **Request a Password**
- *Report a breach of license:* **Cate Hutton**

Questions? Comments?

Selecting and Cataloging OA Resources

http://www.cdlib.org/inside/collect/openaccess.html

Collection Development Process

Open Access Resources at the UC Libraries

Policies and Procedures for Shared Cataloging, Linking, and Management

June 9, 2006

Definition

Open access [1] resources have no financial or legal barriers to access for members of our user community. The following factors must be in evidence:

1. The publication must be available online at no charge to readers or institutions. No subscription can be required for online access.

2. Readers must be permitted to use the material for any lawful purpose, including downloading, copying, making derivative works, distributing, printing, searching, or linking to the full texts of works, crawling for indexing, or passing as data to software.

3. No licensor/licensee relationship shall exist between the publisher or provider of the online publication and the individual user or institution.

Note that some open access resources may provide open access to only portions of their content (e.g., just the backfiles (such as HighWire titles), just the frontfiles, or only some types of articles (some PubMed Central titles). In this case, the 856 field will indicate what content is open access. For example, "Open access to research articles only" will appear in BioMed Central records.

Some open access resources may require registration (i.e., require the user to provide information before access is granted).

Policies

- The **Joint Steering Committee on Shared Resources (JSC)** oversees UC policies for shared cataloging of open access materials.

- Scholarly open access resources (e.g., peer-reviewed journals) are eligible for consideration.

- UC bibliographers must nominate resources for consideration. Unsolicited requests will not be considered.

- Journals must be indexed in a major disciplinary abstracting or indexing service, defined as any Tier 1 abstract or index or the equivalent free service such as PubMed Central. This list is currently available on the **request form**.

- Non-journal open access resources (databases, monographic collections, web sites, map and image collections, etc.) are also eligible for consideration. A brief justification must be submitted for each individual collection according to the evaluation criteria below. Resources delivered through a CDL service (e.g. Luna Insight collections) may be subject to additional technical review by CDL staff after JSC approval.

- Once approved, the Shared Catalog Program (SCP) at UC San Diego will catalog resources and include these records in the existing SCP data streams sent to campuses. A record will appear in the Melvyl Catalog after a campus incorporates that record into their local catalog. Linking via UC-eLinks will be implemented, where possible. A resource liaison may be assigned for each resource or package. SCP will provide regular link checking.

- Requests for cataloging individual items within a collection may also be submitted, using the more detailed project request guidelines on the Shared Cataloging Program website at http://cdlib.org/inside/projects/scp/newprojects.html. Such requests will be considered on a project basis subject to SCP workflow, available cataloging expertise, and other considerations.

- SCP cataloging priorities are outlined more fully on the SCP website at http://cdlib.org/inside/projects/scp.

Evaluation Criteria

Making resources available to the UC community entails considerable cost, whether the resources are licensed or open access. Open access resources should be evaluated according to the same quality use indicators that would be applied to licensed content. Examples of factors to consider include:

- Does the resource satisfy a demonstrable need in ongoing research and/or teaching at UC?
- Is it produced or supported by a recognizable and reputable organization? Is it likely to persist?
- Is it stable and reliable (i.e. free of performance or other problems)?
- Is the interface easy-to-use?
- Does the resource require specialized technology (non-standard browser plug-in, special font support, use of a specialized application, etc)? If so, additional vetting may be required before the resource is approved.

Procedures

	Journals	**Non-Journals (Collections of Monographs, Images, and Maps; Databases and Web Sites)**
Nomination	A UC bibliographer fills out the **request form**. The form gets routed to the Shared Cataloging Program (Becky Culbertson). Becky will batch and route forms to Wendy Parfrey as needed.	UC bibliographers should contact the **appropriate JSC subject liaison** to nominate a resource.
Verification of open access status	UC bibliographers should only submit resources that meet the criteria above. For journals that are automatically approved, the JSC is responsible for verifying the open access status of that resource if that status is challenged.	
Approvals	The following journals are automatically approved and will be routed for cataloging without any approvals process: - Journals indexed in a major disciplinary abstracting and indexing database ; or... - Journals that have an existing SCP record (i.e., this is a new open-access URL with new access, equivalent access, or less content). - Journals listed in the Directory of Open Access Journals (DOAJ). The following require JSC approval: - Journals not indexed in a major disciplinary A&I database. Becky Culbertson will send Wendy Parfrey batches of these titles periodically.	JSC will approve nominated resources as part of their regular operations. Resources delivered through a CDL service (e.g., Luna Insight databases) may be subject to additional technical review by CDL staff. When a nominated resource is approved, JSC will inform SCP and UC-eLinks staff so they can begin cataloging and linking, respectively.

Cataloging	- To the extent possible, SCP catalogers will assign BibPurls (PIDs) and add them to the OCLC record.
	- Non-journals will be cataloged at the collection-level only unless requested otherwise. Requests for item-level cataloging will be considered on a project basis following SCP guidelines at http://cdlib.org/inside/projects/scp/newprojects.html .
	- Cataloging hook in 793:
	    - "Open access resource freely available; selected by the UC libraries"
	    - When only portions of the resource are open access, the	

http://www.cdlib.org/inside/collect/openaccess.html

	appropriate wording will be added to the 856 $z. Addition of such wording will be added reactively, i.e., when SCP is advised or discovers that portions of the resource are not open access.
Linking	• To the extent possible, article-level linking via UC-eLinks will be created for all open access resources.
Management	• Open access resources will not be added to the existing CDL MIS database, but may be included in a future ERM system. • The CDL will attempt to troubleshoot access issues when reported. • Some larger groups of open access resources (e.g., BioMedCentral) may require a resource liaison.

[1] Definition compiled by Dave Fisher, UC San Diego. Sources include: Bethesda Statement on Open Access Publishing; Budapest Open Access Initiative; SPARC Open Access Newsletter, issue 64, August 4, 2003; DOAJ web site; Creative Commons Attribution — Non-Commercial — shareAlike License 1.0.

Document owner: **Wendy Parfrey**
Last reviewed: June 8, 2006
URL: http://www.cdlib.org/inside/collect/openaccess.html

Questions? Comments?

http://www.umanitoba.ca/libraries/media/422_Internet_materials.pdf

Policy:	**422**
Subject:	**INTERNET MATERIALS**
Approved by:	LMAC

Contact:	Coordinator, Collections Management	**Approved:** April 9, 1998
Prepared by:	Task Force on the Internet and	**Revised:** March 21, 2002
	and the Collections	February 17, 2005

Purpose

The objective of this policy is to provide guidelines for the collection and incorporation of relevant Internet materials into the UML online catalogue. For procedures related to the acquisition and cataloguing of NETDOC resources see CAP Policy 435 - NETDOC Purchase Procedures.

Definitions

1. **Internet resource.** An Internet resource is an electronic work in a machine-readable format, which is accessible through a wide-area network. This is in contrast to a direct access electronic work issued in a physical carrier, e.g., CD-ROMs, computer disks (floppy disks), etc., accessible only in a stand-alone PC or through a local area network.[1]

2. **UML online catalogue.** The University of Manitoba Libraries' online catalogue consists of the BISON database of MARC records. It is accessed through a Web-based interface (U of M's implementation of Sirsi's Web 2).

3. **URL: Uniform Resource Locator.** The URL provides a World Wide Web address that specifies the location of a resource on the Internet. This address is used to create a hypertext link in the Web-based interface of the UML online catalogue. This link when clicked takes the user directly to the resource.

4. **Full text/full image.** A monograph is considered to be full text/full image when the entire content, including images, of the print title is available online. A periodical is considered to be full text when the text of all articles in a print issue are available online and the full text of all the issues in at least one volume are available online. Born digital works are considered to be full text/full image.

---

[1] This is based on the definition of Internet resources in Dillon, Martin and Erik Jul. 1996. Cataloguing Internet resources, the convergence of libraries and Internet resources. <u>Cataloging & classification quarterly</u>, v.22, no.3/4 and the definition of direct access computer files in <u>Anglo-American cataloguing rules, second edition, 1988 revision</u>.

http://www.umanitoba.ca/libraries/media/422_Internet_materials.pdf

Policy 422:   INTERNET MATERIALS   422.2

Preamble

The Internet includes a wide range of resources of varying quality. High quality Internet resources relevant to the mission of the University of Manitoba Libraries in its support of teaching and research programs of the university will be selected for inclusion in the UML online catalogue. The best way to choose Internet resources of high quality is through title by title selection according to current collection management policies, guidelines, and statements.[2]

Policy Statement

Selection, retention, archiving and deselection of Internet resources within current UML collection policy guidelines rest with bibliographers/unit heads who have designated responsibility for specific areas. This policy does not apply to individual library's home pages or to Web-based NETDOC materials.

Selection[3]

1.   The following categories of Internet material may be selected for inclusion in the UML online catalogue:

     a)   full text electronic resources, including monographs, serials, etc.;
     b)   online parts of print works, e.g., a print work with statistical tables only available on a Web site;
     c)   multimedia resources (works including images, videos, and sound, with or without text).

2.   The following categories of Internet resources will in general be excluded from the UML online catalogue:

     a)   search engines, e.g., Google;
     b)   directories/indexes to the Internet itself, e.g., Yahoo.

3.   Printed copies of electronic resources documents are accepted for inclusion in the UML online catalogue only in exceptional circumstances when a bibliographer or unit head determines that the material should be permanently retained and warrants the additional cost of printing, storing and binding the document.

---

[2] Demas, Samuel and others. 1995. The Internet and collection development, mainstreaming selection of Internet resources. Library resources and technical services, v.39(3), p.280.

[3] See Appendix A for suggested selection guidelines.

Policy 422:   INTERNET MATERIALS   422.3

Funding

Those Internet resources which require payment (license fees, subscription fees, etc.) are funded from the unit libraries' acquisition funds (operating or gift).

Access/Cataloguing

1.   Access to Internet resources will be provided in the UML online catalogue by catalogue records which will include 856 fields for Electronic location and access. 856 fields generally include URLs.

2.   Catalogue records for print titles which have parts available only on the Internet will also contain URLs for those parts and notes identifying the parts.

3.   Internet resources will be identified in the UML online catalogue by the equivalent of a library location name: Internet resources.

4.   All Internet resources should be made available through UM Links whenever possible.

Retention/Maintenance of URLs

1.   Deselection of Internet resources will in general follow the same policies applicable to deselection of other categories of materials. (see CAP Policy 315: Discarding of Library Materials)

2.   URLs of Internet resources in catalogue records will be monitored to ensure their continued functionality.

3.   Questions regarding malfunctioning URL's should be directed to the Electronic Resources unit.

Procedures Applicable to All Units

1.   Requests for Internet resources (whether free or requiring payment) are sent by email to the Electronic Resources unit with the title and URL. Requests for paid resources should also include fund number, depth of coverage and number of simultaneous users desired (where applicable).

2.   Electronic Resources staff obtain license agreements for Internet Resources and complete a preliminary review of related materials, noting areas of special technical interest or legal conditions. These licenses are then forwarded to the Head of

Policy 422:   **INTERNET MATERIALS**   422.4

Electronic Resources for detailed review. The Head executes changes to licenses, ensuring compliance with all legal requirements and intended use, elimination of foreseeable breaches of contract, and indemnification. Licenses that require amendments or signature are signed by the Head and routed for signature to the publisher or vendor. Licenses which are approved without changes are accepted online or signed as required. The final version of all license agreements are printed and filed in Electronic Resources.

3.   Once activation of an Internet Resource has been confirmed by Electronic Resources, the Head of Electronic Resources advises the Electronic Journals Distribution List of each new title or change in title. These announcements serve to request promotion, cataloguing by Bibliographic Control or NJMHSL Resource Management, as appropriate, and technical updates by LETS, in order to establish and maintain the necessary access points.

    a)   In the case of bibliographic databases with unconfirmed or questionable full-text content, Electronic Resources will distribute a list of available journals to subject bibliographers. Bibliographers will then examine the journals in the database and request specific titles for cataloguing. The Head of Electronic Resources will advise the Electronic Journals Distribution List of new titles selected by the subject bibliographers; this notice will serve to request promotion and cataloguing by Bibliographic Control.

4.   Upon notification by the Head of the Electronic Resources unit, Bibliographic Control enters catalogue records with functioning links to Internet resources into the UML online catalogue.

    a)   Electronic Resources will add the titles to the UM Links whenever possible.

Policy 422:   INTERNET MATERIALS   422.5

Appendix 1.1

GUIDELINES FOR SELECTION OF INTERNET RESOURCES:[4]

(Note: These criteria are intended to assist in the evaluation and selection process. Resources can be acceptable without meeting all of the criteria listed.)

Quality and Content

Credible source as indicated by:

- Content peer-reviewed by experts in the field.
- Produced as part of the mission of a national or international organization.
- Developed by an academic institution or commercial enterprise with an established reputation in topical area.
- Resource is indexed or archived electronically (if appropriate).

Importance of resource as demonstrated by availability:

- Resource is available from or pointed to by multiple Internet sites.
- Database or document is reproduced in multiple formats (print, online, CD-ROM, etc.).

Content is comprehensive or unique:

- Resource is known or can be shown to cover subject area well.
- Information would likely be unavailable to clients otherwise.
- Resource is full text.
- Internet version of the resource is the most current.

Content of Internet version is complete or meets client needs:

- Internet document or database mirrors that available from other sources or in other formats.
- If the timespan or the content of the Internet version of the resource is limited, the resource is still of use.
- Because of subject area, increased demand is likely in the future (e.g., health care reform).

The resource stays current through regular updates or demonstrates ongoing maintenance.

---

[4] (adapted for U of M from Guidelines for Internet resource selection by Gregory F. Pratt, Patrick Flannery, and Cassandra L. D. Perkins, C&RL News, March 1996)

Policy 422:   INTERNET MATERIALS   422.6

Appendix 1.2

Relevancy

- Resource is related to teaching and research programs of the University of Manitoba.
- Library personnel or client recommended resource.
- Access is provided by other local institutions or major universities.
- Usage data indicate client interest or demand.

Ease of Use

- If a logon sequence is required, it can be scripted or automated for clients.
- If searchable, searching is similar to that of other available Internet resources.
- If a unique interface is used, the resource is of sufficient importance that client access is still worthwhile.
- If needed, user help files or resource description files are readily available.
- The amount of user support required from Reference Desk or LETS Help Desk is minimal or acceptable.

Cost and Copyright

- Any subscription or access costs are reasonable and justifiable.
- It is simple to comply with restrictions on duplication or dissemination of information from the resource.

Hardware and Software

- Providing access requires little or no change in existing or planned hardware and software resources.

http://www.lib.virginia.edu/acquisitions/other_procedures/websites.html

Acquisitions Department

help us grOW   home   general info   services   collections   subject guides   index   QUESTIONS?

About US

Acquisitions Staff Resources

Collections/Selectors' Resources
   Collection Development Tools
   Collections Group
   Forms
   Glossary of Library Terms
   Policies & Procedures
   Publisher Package & Memberships
   Selectors & Areas of Selection
   Trials (Online Databases)
   Vendors (by Country)
   Vendors Online (Alphabetical)
   VIVA
   New Acquisitions

Copyright Information

Selecting Web Sites for Cataloging

Selecting Web Sites for Cataloging

Ad Hoc Committee On Digital Access: Final Report (1998)

" Access should be provided to electronic information created, purchased or acquired contractually by the library. Access to electronic information which is not created, purchased or acquired contractually (eg. free web sites), should be provided when selected by a subject selector."

http://www.lib.virginia.edu/cataloging/policies/local/digital.html

Guidelines for Selecting Web Sites for Cataloging

1. The site must be relevant to departmental teaching and research.

2. Its content should be scholarly, clearly organized, and easy to search.

3. It should be maintained and up-to-date, and largely complete rather than under construction.

4. Emphasis should be on sites offering full content rather than partial summaries of content.

5. Sites with password requirements should not be cataloged.

Cataloging Request forms

http://www.lib.virginia.edu/cataloging/policies/forms/web-req.html
(Everything except serials)

http://www.lib.virginia.edu/cataloging/policies/forms/web-ser.html
(Serials only)

Cataloging contacts

Electronic cataloging in general: Erin Stalberg, stalberg@virginia.edu; 982-2854

E-journals: Deej Baker, dbc@virginia.edu; 924-4958

E-journals (backup): Cary Coleman, rcc6qa@virginia.edu; 924-3288

(These guidelines reviewed by Collections Group July, 2004)

http://www.lib.virginia.edu/cataloging/policies/forms/web-ser.html

UNIVERSITY VIRGINIA LIBRARY **Cataloging Services**

SEARCH VIRGO CATALOG

Go!

GO TO VIRGO DATABASES

help us grOW | home | general info | services | collections | subject guides | index | QUESTIONS?

About the Cataloging Services Department

Request, Maintenance and Statistics Forms

Policies and Procedures
Cataloging Procedures Manual
Class Archives
WorkFlows Tips
Reports

Catalogers' Resources

Serials / Periodicals

Library Cataloging Request Form

for Adding Free Serial Internet Resources to VIRGO Online Catalog

Library Collection Selectors: please use this form to add **serial** titles for Internet resources to the library's online catalog. Serials selcted should be full-text and not require the use of individual passwords, etc.

All fields should be filled in with the exception of those labelled optional.

Bibliographic Information:

Title

URL:

Licensing:
No licensing

Full text holdings begin with:

Relevant Comments (optional): Include such things as availability of print, etc.:

Selector Information:

Selector's Name:

Email Address:

Phone:

submit | clear

Coordination of Electronic Journal Activities
Urban campuses and Pullman campus
April 28, 2006

SUBSCRIBED TITLES

Vancouver – because of the volume of electronic journals,
- Vancouver will license, process and make links available in Griffin to their electronic journals. Linking will be done through the III Electronic Resource Management module.
- Vancouver will notify the SFX KnowledgeBase manager* in Pullman of new titles for inclusion and activation in SFX. The information needed is the title, ISSN, dates of coverage and who has access. This will provide linking from source databases as well as listing in the SFX electronic A-Z list.

Energy Library, Spokane and TriCities - Because of the small number of electronic journals dealt with at these campuses, Pullman Collections and Technical Services unit will handle activation/registration, Griffin linking, and SFX activation.

Procedure:
- Campus will purchase and license
- Send an Electronic Product Purchase Request form prominently marked with your campus name

http://www.systems.wsu.edu/bin/libdocs/librarians/E-PurchaseRequestForm.doc

to Serials and Electronic Resources (SER) unit acquisitions staff person** along with copies of any documentation about the title. This might include license, terms of agreement, relevant emails, contact information for technical support and customer service.
- The Electronic Product Purchase Request form will be processed with a top priority according to our usual work flow.
  - o SFX will be activated to provide linking from source databases and inclusion in the SFX electronic journal list
  - o Resource and license records will be created if needed
  - o Links will be added to Griffin via ERM
- SER will notify the purchasing campus when the title is available in Griffin

FREE TITLES

All campuses send Electronic Product Purchase forms to Pullman SER acquisitions staff person for processing. We automatically add free titles from the following suppliers:

Bioline

http://www.wsulibs.wsu.edu/TSD/ejournalprocedures4-28-06.doc

BioMed Central (journals with complete free full text not just selected)
Directory of Online Access Journals (DOAJ)
EMIS
Highwire
Internet Scientific Publications
JSTAGE
National Academy Press (eBooks)
PubMed Central
Scielo
University of California Press Free (eBooks)

**Chris Benson as of 2006
*Janet Chisman as of 2006

Institutional Repositories

http://escholarship.bc.edu/

home
about
policies
help
my account
notify me

Search
Advanced Search

Browse research & scholarship

Browse research and scholarship by

- research unit, center, or department
- personal researcher pages
- author
- journals and peer-reviewed series
- theses and dissertations

This repository is a pilot project of the eScholarship@BC initiative of the **Boston College Libraries**. Research and scholarly output included here has been selected and deposited on behalf of individual university departments and centers. The goal of the repository is to maximize research visibility, influence and benefit by encouraging Boston College authors to archive and distribute online both unpublished work and peer-reviewed publications in an open-access environment. For more information, contact **Mark Caprio**.

paper of the day

Christ, Israel, and salvation according to the Summa Theologiae of St. Thomas Aquinas

by Matthew Webb Levering
Boston College Dissertations and Theses

Search all of the papers

Go

2532 full-text downloads of repository content in the last week.

HOME | SEARCH | HELP | MY ACCOUNT | ABOUT | NOTIFY

eJournal Pilot Project

HOME   ABOUT   LOGIN   REGISTER   SEARCH

Home > Open Journal Systems

Open Journal Systems

OPEN JOURNAL SYSTEMS

Journal Help

USER

Username

Password

Remember me

Sign In

The UBC Library is conducting a pilot project to host faculty ejournals. We are providing access to server space and to the open source OJS (Open Journal Systems) software to UBC faculty members who are editing or supporting Open Access electronic journals.

As part of our pilot project, we are interested in expanding our hosting service to include additional ejournals. Please contact Bronwen Sprout, Digital Initiatives Librarian, University Archives if you are interested in being part of the project, or for more information.

JOURNAL CONTENT

Search

All

Search

Canadian Journal of Midwifery Research and Practice -Revue Canadienne de la Recherche et de la Practique Sage-femme

VIEW JOURNAL | CURRENT ISSUE | REGISTER

Nodalist

A UBC Library in-house journal that discusses the transition to an on-line Library.

VIEW JOURNAL | CURRENT ISSUE | REGISTER

The Journal of Practice Education

VIEW JOURNAL | CURRENT ISSUE | REGISTER

BC Educational Leadership Research

VIEW JOURNAL | CURRENT ISSUE | REGISTER

TCI (Transnational Curriculum Inquiry)

VIEW JOURNAL | CURRENT ISSUE | REGISTER

New Proposals: Journal of Marxism and Interdisciplinary Inquiry

VIEW JOURNAL | CURRENT ISSUE | REGISTER

http://repositories.cdlib.org/escholarship/

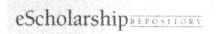 

HOME   HELP   MY ACCOUNT   ABOUT   SEARCH

eScholarship

Search all 17,969 papers

Notify me of new papers
via Email or RSS

Browse research and scholarship

- Campus
- Research unit, center, or department
- Journals and peer-reviewed series
- Seminar series
- Postprints

Last week...
26,021 full-text downloads of repository content

To date...
5,823,410 full-text downloads

The repository is a service of the eScholarship initiative of the California Digital Library. Research and scholarly output included here has been selected and deposited by the individual University of California units.

Paper of the day

Moods in everyday situations: Effects of menstrual cycle, work, and stress hormones
by Dmitry M. Davydov, David Shapiro, Iris B. Goldstein, and Aleksandra Chicz-DeMet

Postprints, University of California,

Top downloads

Top ten papers, all time

Top ten recent papers

Open Archives Compliant

eScholarship is a service of the California Digital Library

powered by
bepress

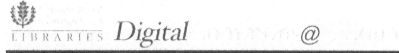

home

about

help

for authors

using and citing

my account

notify me

contacts

University of Connecticut Libraries

Search   Advanced
Search

RSS

POW

Browse research & scholarship

Browse research and scholarship by

> **research unit, center, or department**
> **theses and dissertations**
> **author**
> **personal researcher pages**

DigitalCommons@UConn is a project coordinated by the Institutional Repository Team within the UConn Libraries. It is an electronic repository of the intellectual output of the University of Connecticut community, and represents a way for UConn to organize, store and preserve its research in digital form in a single unified location. For more information, email **digitalcommons@uconn.edu**.

HOME | ABOUT | HELP | MY ACCOUNT | NOTIFY ME | SEARCH

paper of the day

Trust, moral ties, and social responsibility

by Jessica Prata Miller
ETD Collection for University of Connecticut

703 full-text downloads of repository content in the last week.

There are 4004 documents in the repository as of today.

FLORIDA STATE UNIVERSITY

http://digitool3.lib.fsu.edu/R/

Search | Results | Previous Searches | Search Bases | My Space   Login   End Session | Help
Guest

Welcome to the FSU Libraries Digital Library Center Institutional Repository

This respository provides access to a variety of FSU Libraries DLC digital collections from images to Encoded Archival Description (EAD) finding aids to text including "open access" electronic theses and dissertations (ETD) for the scholarly communications, research, and learning communities.

Use the Simple or Advanced Search form to search for a specific item or click on the collection links to browse the collections.

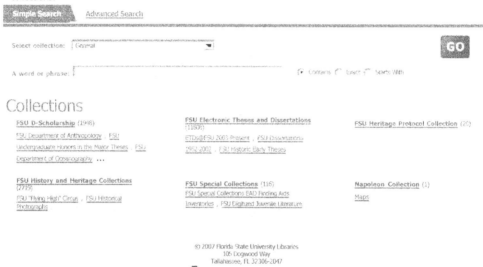

Collections

FSU D-Scholarship (1948)
FSU Department of Anthropology , FSU Undergraduate Honors in the Major Theses , FSU Department of Oceanography ...

FSU History and Heritage Collections (2719)
FSU "Flying High" Circus , FSU Historical Photographs

FSU Electronic Theses and Dissertations (11508)
ETDs@FSU 2003-Present , FSU Dissertations 1952-2002 , FSU Historic Early Theses

FSU Special Collections (116)
FSU Special Collections EAD Finding Aids Inventories , FSU Digitized Juvenile Literature

FSU Heritage Protocol Collection (20)

Napoleon Collection (1)
Maps

© 2007 Florida State University Libraries
105 Dogwood Way
Tallahassee, FL 32306-2047

FSU DigiTool 3.1 Comments/Questions

ScholarWorks@UMass Amherst

Home

About

My Account

Notify Me

UMass Amherst Libraries

UMass Amherst

Search »

Advanced Search

RSS

For Authors

Help

Contact Us

POWERED BY
bepress

Browse Research & Scholarship

Browse research and scholarship by:

- Doctoral Dissertations
- Journals and Peer-Reviewed Series
- Masters Theses
- Personal Researcher Pages
- Research Centers and Institutes
- School, College, or Department
- University of Massachusetts Press

ScholarWorks@UMass Amherst is a digital repository for the research and scholarly output of members of the University of Massachusetts Amherst community, administered by the UMass Amherst Libraries.

Paper of the Day

Synthesis and characterization of poly(gamma-glutamic acid) hydrogels and their application in slow-release of porcine somatotropin

by Kesuo Fan
Electronic Doctoral Dissertations for UMass Amherst

Search all 4175 papers

Go

385 full-text downloads of repository content in the last week.

Frequently downloaded papers
Most recent papers

ScholarWorks: Home | Search | Help | My Account | About | Notify Me

Research Laboratory for Electronics (RLE)
School of Engineering
Science, Technology & Society
Singapore-MIT Alliance (SMA)
Sloan School of Management
Synthetic Biology
Systems Design & Management
Technology and Policy Program
Warren M. Rohsenow Heat and Mass Transfer Laboratory

vision · collaboration · invention

Copyright © 2002 MIT and Hewlett-Packard - Feedback

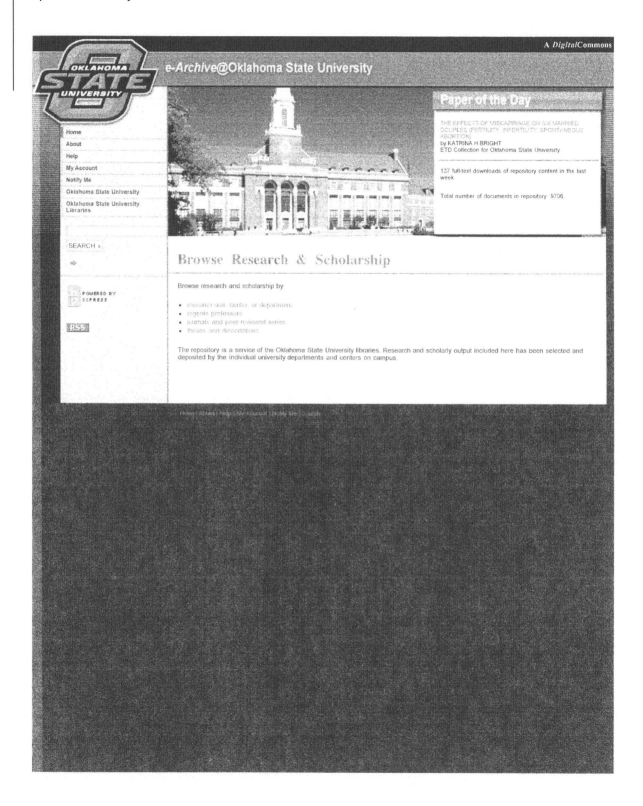

RU**core** ⊁RUcore Tools

RU**core** Tools

RUcore tools are designed to make it easy for Rutgers faculty and their collaborators to participate in the Rutgers Community Repository.

RUcore is developing tools that faculty can apply to their research projects to organize information and make it available to the worldwide community of researchers.

RUcore develops tools for the repository and in collaboration with RU departments and individuals.

Under Development:

Electronic theses and dissertations application
In collaboration with the Graduate School - New Brunswick, a service to automate the workflow of submitting a thesis or dissertation to the graduate school, as well as to build a collection of electronic theses and dissertations that can be browsed by school or department, as well as by subject, author, etc. is under development.

Custom collection search and display
This tool, which will be available in v 4.0, will allow any individual or project to easily add collection searching to a home page, electronic CV, or project website, so that project resources belonging to that collection can be searched and displayed. The search and retrieval will be automatically up to date with any resources that the faculty member, department or project adds.

Current Tools:

Workflow Management System
The most important tool is the Workflow Management System-a web-based graphical user interface for uploading digital objects (images, data sets, audio files, video files, digital text, etc.) and creating metadata to describe and manage those objects.

The WMS supports two roles: the **administrator**, who selects vocabularies and designs **metadata templates** that provide default information for many data elements, to speed up the metadata creation process, and the team member, who uploads objects and creates metadata, using the **metadata templates**.

http://rucore.libraries.rutgers.edu/services/

An interactive demonstration of the WMS will soon be available.

In the meantime, you can take a tour of the WMS by reading the <u>WMS Users' Guide</u>, which includes step-by-step instructions and screen shots.

The WMS supports the RUcore data model, with metadata to describe and manage digital objects. You can find definitions and examples for all the metadata data elements in the Repository Metadata Guidelines.

WMS Documentation:

<u>WMS Users' Guide</u>
<u>Repository Metadata Guidelines</u>

For more information about WMS, <u>contact the WMS project manager</u>.

E-Journal platform

RUcore has developed an electronic open journal platform that establishes a peer-review process, a web-based presentation platform for searching or browsing journal issues and an article-level archiving strategy that maintains each article in the RUcore repository. Current journals include <u>Pragmatic Case Studies in Psychotherapy</u>, <u>The Electronic Journal of Boundary Elements</u>, <u>Journal of Rutgers University Libraries</u> and the <u>Rutgers Scholar: an Electronic Bulletin of Undergraduate Research</u>. If you are interested in using RUL's open journal system to publish an e-journal, <u>contact the project manager</u>.

Web archiving tool

Websites can be encapsulated, with their site navigation and image files intact, for an archived "snapshot" of the website at a specific date and time. <u>Contact the project manager</u> for more information.

Open Archives Initiative (OAI) facility

Supports sharing resources with other initiatives via harvesting from RU**core**.

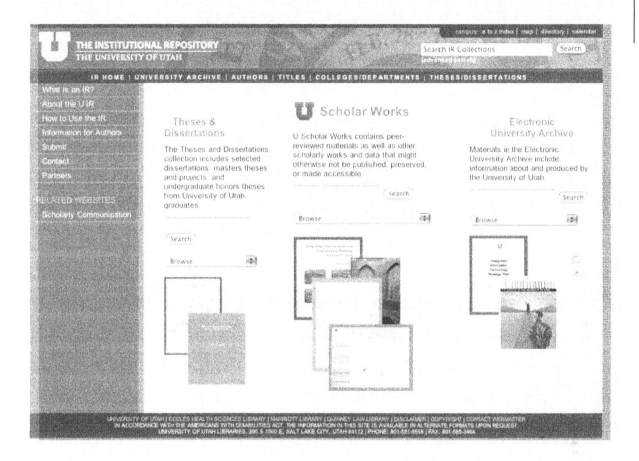

WAYNE STATE UNIVERSITY

http://digitalcommons.wayne.edu/

WAYNE STATE
UNIVERSITY *Digital*Commons@Wayne State

Home

About

Help

My Account

Notify Me

Wayne State University

Search

[   ]

SEARCH »

» Advanced Search

POWERED BY
BEPRESS

RSS

Browse Research & Scholarship

Browse research and scholarship by:

- research unit, center, or department
- journals and peer-reviewed series
- theses and dissertations

The repository is a service of the Wayne State University libraries. Research and scholarly output included here has been selected and deposited by the individual university departments and centers on campus.

Paper of the Day

Gender-related perceptions of parental treatment of Arabic speaking fifth-grade urban students

by Therese Jiries Smith
ETD Collection for Wayne State University

Search all 3023 papers

[   ] [Go]

199 full-text downloads of repository content in the last week.

Home | About | Help | My Account | Notify Me | Search

SELECTED RESOURCES

DOCUMENTS

Books and Journal Articles

Anderson, Rick. "Open Access—Clear Benefits, Hidden Costs." Learned Publishing 20, no. 2 (2007): 83–84.

Anderson, Rick. "Open Access in the Real World." College & Research Libraries News 65, no. 4 (2004): 206–08.

Bailey, Charles W., Jr. Open Access Bibliography: Liberating Scholarly Literature with E-Prints and Open Access Journals. Washington, DC: Association of Research Libraries, 2005.

Blummer, Barbara. "Biz of Acq—Opportunities for Librarians with Open Access Publishing." Against the Grain 17, no. 6 (2006): 65–68.

Bosc, Hélène, and Stevan Harnad. "In a Paperless World a New Role for Academic Libraries: Providing Open Access." Learned Publishing 18, no. 2 (2005): 95–99.

Canepi, Kitti, et al. "Open Access and Conscious Selection." Serials Librarian 52, no. 3 (2007): 331–34.

Corrado, Edward M. "The Importance of Open Access, Open Source, and Open Standards for Libraries." Issues in Science & Technology Librarianship 42 (2005): N.PAG.

Crawford, Walt. "Open Access and Survivable Libraries." EContent 28, no. 6 (2005): 42.

Daniels, Tim, and Elizabeth Winter. "What can the Role of Technical Services be in Managing Institutional Repositories?" Charleston Conference Proceedings 2005. Ed. Beth R Bernhardt, et al. Westport, Conn.: Libraries Unlimited, 2006.

Donovan, Georgie, and Karen Estlund. "New Librarians and Scholarly Communication." College & Research Libraries News 68, no. 3 (2007): 155–62.

Drake, Miriam A. "Open Access." Searcher 15, no. 7 (2007): 51–54.

Grogg, Jill E. "Linking Users to Open Access." Searcher 13, no. 4 (2005): 52–56.

Hixson, Carol. "If We Build It, Will They Come (Eventually)? Scholarly Communication and Institutional Repositories." Serials Librarian 50, no. 1 (2006): 197–209.

Ho, Adrian K., and Charles W. Bailey, Jr. "Open Access Webliography." Reference Services Review 33, no. 3 (2005): 346–64.

Jacobs, Neil. Open Access: Key Strategic, Technical and Economic Aspects. Oxford: Chandos, 2006.

Koehler, Amy E. C. "Some Thoughts on the Meaning of Open Access for University Library Technical Services." Serials Review 32, no. 1 (2006): 17–21.

Kwasik, Hanna, and Pauline O. Fulda. "Open Access and Scholarly Communication—A Selection of Key Web Sites." Issues in Science & Technology Librarianship 43 (2005): N.PAG.

Morris, Sally. "When is a Journal Not a Journal? A Closer Look at the DOAJ." Learned Publishing 19, no. 1 (2006): 73–76.

Morrison, Heather G. "The Dramatic Growth of Open Access: Implications and Opportunities for Resource Sharing." Journal of Interlibrary Loan, Document Supply & Electronic Reserves 16, no. 3 (2006): 95–107.

"Open Access from the Librarian's Perspective." Library & Information Update 5, no. 11 (2006): 6–7.

"OpenDOAR or Directory of Open Access Repositories." Information Services & Use 25, no. 2 (2005): 109–11.

Pelizzari, Eugenio. "Harvesting for Disseminating: Open Archives and the Role of Academic Libraries." Acquisitions Librarian 17, no. 33 (2005): 35–51.

"Roles Shifting as OA Expands." Library & Information Update 5, no. 11 (2006): 6–7.

Rowland, Fytton. "How do we Provide Access to the Content of Scholarly Research Information?" Serials 18, no. 3 (2005): 218–29.

Sale, Arthur. "The Acquisition of Open Access Research Articles." First Monday 10 (2006): 5–.

Schmidt, Krista D., Pongracz Sennyey, and Timothy V. Carstens. "New Roles for a Changing Environment: Implications of Open Access for Libraries." College & Research Libraries 66, no. 5 (2005): 407–16.

Schmidt, Krista, and Nancy Newsome. "The Changing Landscape of Serials: Open Access Journals in the Public Catalog." Serials Librarian 52, no. 1 (2007): 119–33.

Schwartz, Charles A. "Reassessing Prospects for the Open Access Movement." College & Research Libraries 66, no. 6 (2005): 488–95.

Sotudeh, Hajar, and Abbas Horri. "Tracking Open Access Journals Evolution: Some Considerations in Open Access Data Collection Validation." Journal of the American Society for Information Science & Technology 58, no. 11 (2007): 1578–85.

Thomas, Sarah E. "Publishing Solutions for Contemporary Scholars: The Library as Innovator and Partner." Library Hi Tech 24, no. 4 (2006): 563–73.

University of Houston Libraries Institutional Repository Task Force. Institutional Repositories SPEC Kit 292. Washington, DC: Association of Research Libraries, July 2006.

Van Orsdel, Lee C., and Kathleen Born. "Serial Wars." Library Journal 132, no. 7 (2007): 43–48.

Van Orsdel, Lee C. "The State of Scholarly Communications: An Environmental Scan of Emerging Issues, Pitfalls, and Possibilities." Serials Librarian 52, no.1 (2007): 191–209.

Walters, William H., and Esther Isabelle Wilder. "The Cost Implications of Open-Access Publishing in the Life Sciences." Bioscience 57, no. 7 (2007): 619–25.

Walters, William H. "Institutional Journal Costs in an Open Access Environment." Journal of the American Society for Information Science & Technology 58, no. 1 (2007): 108–20.

Willinsky, John. The Access Principle: The Case for Open Access to Research and Scholarship. Cambridge, Mass.: MIT Press, 2006.

Wood, Elizabeth H. "Open Access Publishing: Implications for Libraries." Journal of Electronic Resources in Medical Libraries 2, no. 2 (2005): 1–12.

Yiotis, Kristin. "The Open Access Initiative: A New Paradigm for Scholarly Communications." Information Technology & Libraries 24, no. 4 (2005): 157–62.

Zhang, Sha Li. "The Flavors of Open Access." OCLC Systems & Services: International Digital Library Perspectives 23, no. 3 (2007): 229–34.

Web Sites

OA Librarian: Open access resources by and for librarians
http://oalibrarian.blogspot.com/

Peter Suber's Open Access Overview, http://www.earlham.edu/~peters/fos/overview.htm

and Open Access News http://www.earlham.edu/~peters/fos/fosblog.html

Budapest Open Access Initiative
http://www.soros.org/openaccess/read.shtml

Bethesda Statement on Open Access Publishing
http://www.earlham.edu/~peters/fos/bethesda.htm

Berlin Declaration on Open Access to Knowledge in the Sciences and Humanities
http://oa.mpg.de/openaccess-berlin/berlindeclaration.html

Charles W. Bailey, Jr.'s Key Open Access Concepts
http://www.escholarlypub.com/oab/keyoaconcepts.htm

Open Access Bibliography: Liberating Scholarly Literature with E-Prints and Open Access Journals
(Charles W. Bailey, Jr)
http://www.escholarlypub.com/oab/

Open Access—A Primer (Mark E. Funk)
http://www.mlanet.org/pdf/resources/oa_primer_mfunk.pdf

Create Change
http://www.createchange.org/index.html

SPARC (Scholarly Publishing and Academic Resources Coalition)
http://www.arl.org/sparc/about/index.html

Open Archives Initiative
http://www.openarchives.org/

Directory of Open Access Journals (DOAJ)
http://www.doaj.org/

Directory of Open Access Repositories – OpenDOAR
http://www.opendoar.org/

arXiv.org: Open access to 438,783 e-prints in Physics, Mathematics, Computer Science, Quantitative
Biology and Statistics
http://arxiv.org/

Open J-Gate
http://www.openj-gate.org/

OAIster
http://www.oaister.org/

PubMed Central
http://www.pubmedcentral.nih.gov/

Public Library of Science
http://www.plos.org/

BioMed Central
http://www.biomedcentral.com/

Note: All URLs accessed September 25, 2007.

SPEC KIT TITLE LIST

SP125 Tech Svcs Cost Studies	SP083 Approval Plans	SP041 Collection Assessment
SP124 Barcoding of Collections	SP082 Document Delivery Systems	SP040 Skills Training
SP123 Microcomp Software Policies	SP081 Services to the Disabled	SP039 Remote Storage
SP122 End-User Search Svcs	SP080 Specialty Positions	SP038 Collection Dev Policies
SP121 Bibliographic Instruction	SP079 Internships/Job Exchanges	SP037 Theft Detection & Prevent
SP120 Exhibits	SP078 Recruitment-Selection	SP036 Allocation Materials Funds
SP119 Catalog Maintenance Online	SP077 Use of Small Computers	SP035 Preservation of Lib Materials
SP118 Unionization	SP076 Online Biblio Search Svcs	SP034 Determin Indirect Cost Rate
SP117 Gifts & Exchange Function	SP075 Staff Development	SP033 Intergrat Nonprint Media
SP116 Organizing for Preservation	SP074 Fees for Services	SP032 Prep, Present Lib Budget
SP115 Photocopy Services	SP073 External User Services	SP031 Allocation of Resources
SP114 Binding Operations	SP072 Executive Review	SP030 Support Staff, Student Assts
SP113 Preservation Education	SP071 User Surveys: Eval of Lib Svcs	SP029 Systems Function
SP112 Reorg of Tech and Pub Svcs	SP070 Preservation Procedures	SP028 Gifts & Exchange Function
SP111 Cooperative Collection Dev	SP069 Prep Emergencies/Disasters	SP027 Physical Access
SP110 Local Cataloging Policies	SP068 AACR2 Implement Studies	SP026 Bibliographic Access
SP109 Staff Training for Automation	SP067 Affirm Action Programs	SP025 User Statistics and Studies
SP108 Strategic Planning	SP066 Planning Preserv of Lib Mat	SP024 User Surveys
SP107 University Archives	SP065 Retrospective Conversion	SP023 Grievance Policies
SP106 Electronic Mail	SP064 Indirect Cost Rates	SP022 Private Foundations
SP105 Nonbibliographic Dbases	SP063 Collective Bargaining	SP021 Paraprofessionals
SP104 Microcomputers	SP062 Online Biblio Search Svcs	SP020 Managerial Technical Specialists
SP103 Asst/Assoc Dir Position	SP061 Status of Librarians	SP019 Staff Allocations
SP102 Copyright Policies	SP060 Lib Materials Cost Studies	SP018 Staff Development
SP101 User Studies	SP059 Microform Collections	SP017 Library Instruction
SP100 Collection Security	SP058 Goals & Objectives	SP016 Reclassification
SP099 Branch Libraries	SP057 Special Collections	SP015 Goals & Objectives
SP098 Telecommunications	SP056 External Communication	SP014 Performance Review
SP097 Building Renovation	SP055 Internl Com/Staff & Super Role	SP013 Planning Systems
SP096 Online Catalogs	SP054 Internal Com/Policies & Proced	SP012 Acquisition Policies
SP095 Lib Materials Cost Studies	SP053 Performance Appraisal	SP011 Collection Development
SP094 Fund Raising	SP052 Cost Studies & Fiscal Plan	SP010 Leave Policies
SP093 User Instructions for Online Cats	SP051 Professional Development	SP009 Tenure Policies
SP092 Interlibrary Loan	SP050 Fringe Benefits	SP008 Collective Bargaining
SP091 Student Assistants	SP049 Use of Annual Reports	SP007 Personnel Class Schemes
SP090 Integrated Lib Info Systems	SP048 External Fund Raising	SP006 Friends of the Lib Organizations
SP089 Tech Svcs Cost Studies	SP047 Automated Cataloging	SP005 Performance Review
SP088 Corporate Use of Research Libs	SP046 Plan Future of Card Catalog	SP004 Affirmative Action
SP087 Collect Descript/Assessment	SP045 Changing Role Personnel Officer	SP003 A Personnel Organization
SP086 Professional Development	SP044 Automated Acquisitions	SP003 Status of Librarians
SP085 Personnel Classification Sys	SP043 Automated Circulation Sys	SP002 Personnel Survey (flyer only)
SP084 Public Svcs Goals & Objectvs	SP042 Resource Sharing	SP001 Organization Charts

SPEC KIT PRICE INFORMATION

Individual Kits: $35 ARL members/$45 nonmembers, plus shipping and handling.

Individual issues of the Transforming Libraries (TL) subseries: $28, plus shipping and handling.

SHIPPING & HANDLING

U.S.: UPS Ground delivery, $10 per publication.

Canada: UPS Ground delivery, $15 per publication

International and rush orders: Call or e-mail for quote.

PAYMENT INFORMATION

Make check or money order payable in U.S. funds to the **ASSOCIATION OF RESEARCH LIBRARIES,** Federal ID #52-0784198-N. MasterCard and Visa accepted.

SEND ORDERS TO: ARL Publications Distribution Center, P.O. Box 531, Annapolis Junction, MD 20701-0531
phone (301) 362-8196; fax (301) 206-9789; e-mail pubs@arl.org

ORDER ONLINE AT: http://www.arl.org/resources/pubs/index.shtml

1309868

Made in the USA